RUN THE WORLD LIKE A GIRL

KATE GRAHAM
RUN THE WORLD
LIKE A Girl
International Women Leaders
DO YOU KNOW MY NAME?
?
Second
Story
Press

Library and Archives Canada Cataloguing in Publication

Title: Run the world like a girl : international women leaders / Kate Graham.
Other titles: International women leaders
Names: Graham, Kate, 1984- author.
Series: Do you know my name? (Second Story Press (Toronto, Ont.))
Description: Series statement: Do you know my name? ; 5
Identifiers: Canadiana (print) 20250151960 | Canadiana (ebook) 20250152061 | ISBN 9781772604252 (softcover) | ISBN 9781772604269 (EPUB)
Subjects: LCSH: Women heads of state—Biography—Juvenile literature. | LCSH: Heads of state—Biography—Juvenile literature. | LCSH: Women politicians—Biography—Juvenile literature. | LCSH: Politicians—Biography—Juvenile literature. | LCGFT: Biographies.
Classification: LCC HQ1236 .G73 2025 | DDC j305.43/3290922—dc23

Cover and illustrations by Dane Thibeault
Edited by Erin Della Mattia

Printed and bound in Canada

Second Story Press gratefully acknowledges the support of the Ontario Arts Council and the Canada Council for the Arts for our publishing program. We acknowledge the financial support of the Government of Canada through the Canada Book Fund.

Conseil des Arts du Canada
Canada Council for the Arts

Funded by the Government of Canada
Financé par le gouvernement du Canada

Published by
Second Story Press
120 Carlton Street, Suite 412,
Toronto, ON, M5A 4K2
www.secondstorypress.ca

For Jesse, and all parents who believe their girls can do anything

Table of Contents

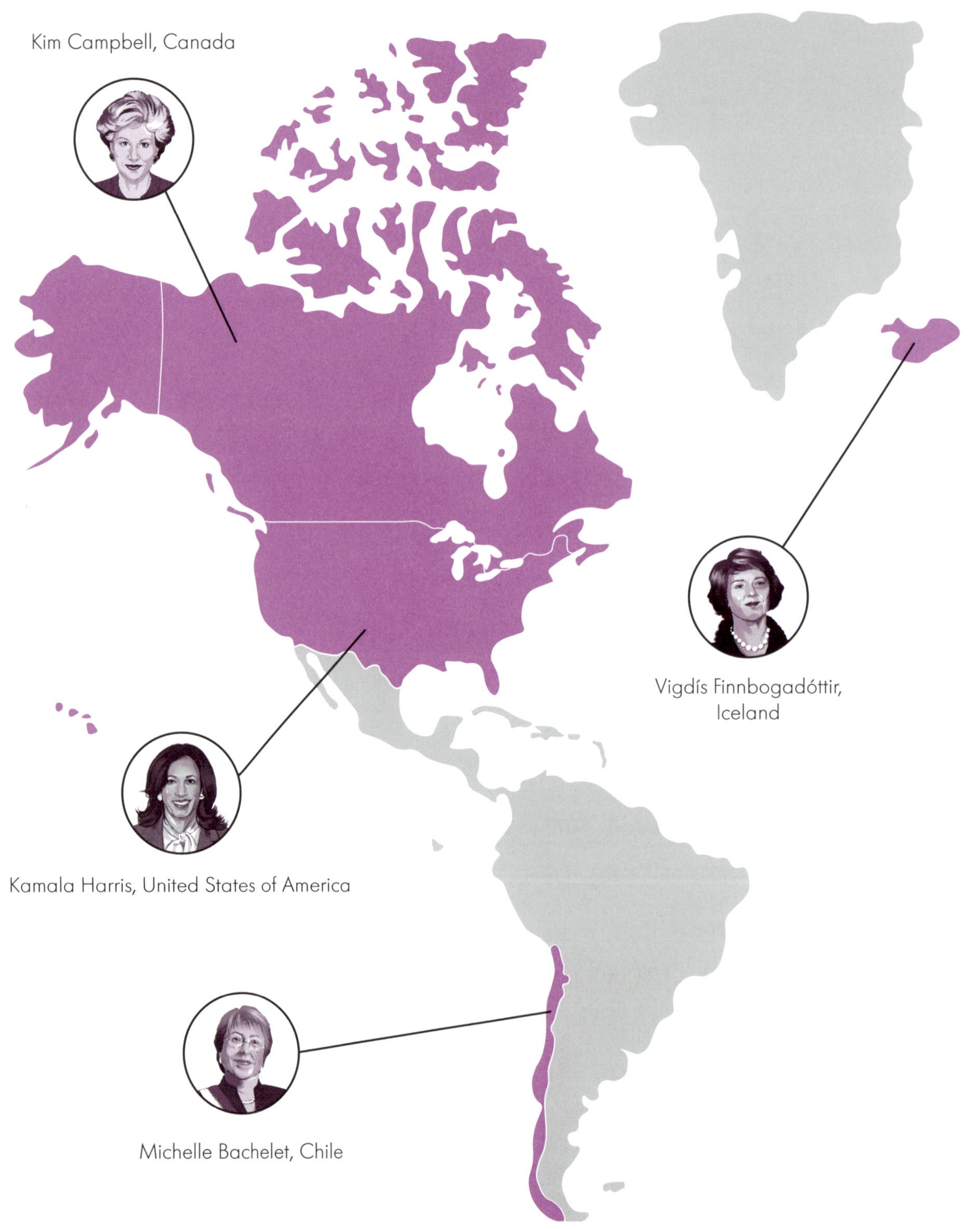
Kim Campbell, Canada
Vigdís Finnbogadóttir,
Iceland
Kamala Harris, United States of America
Michelle Bachelet, Chile

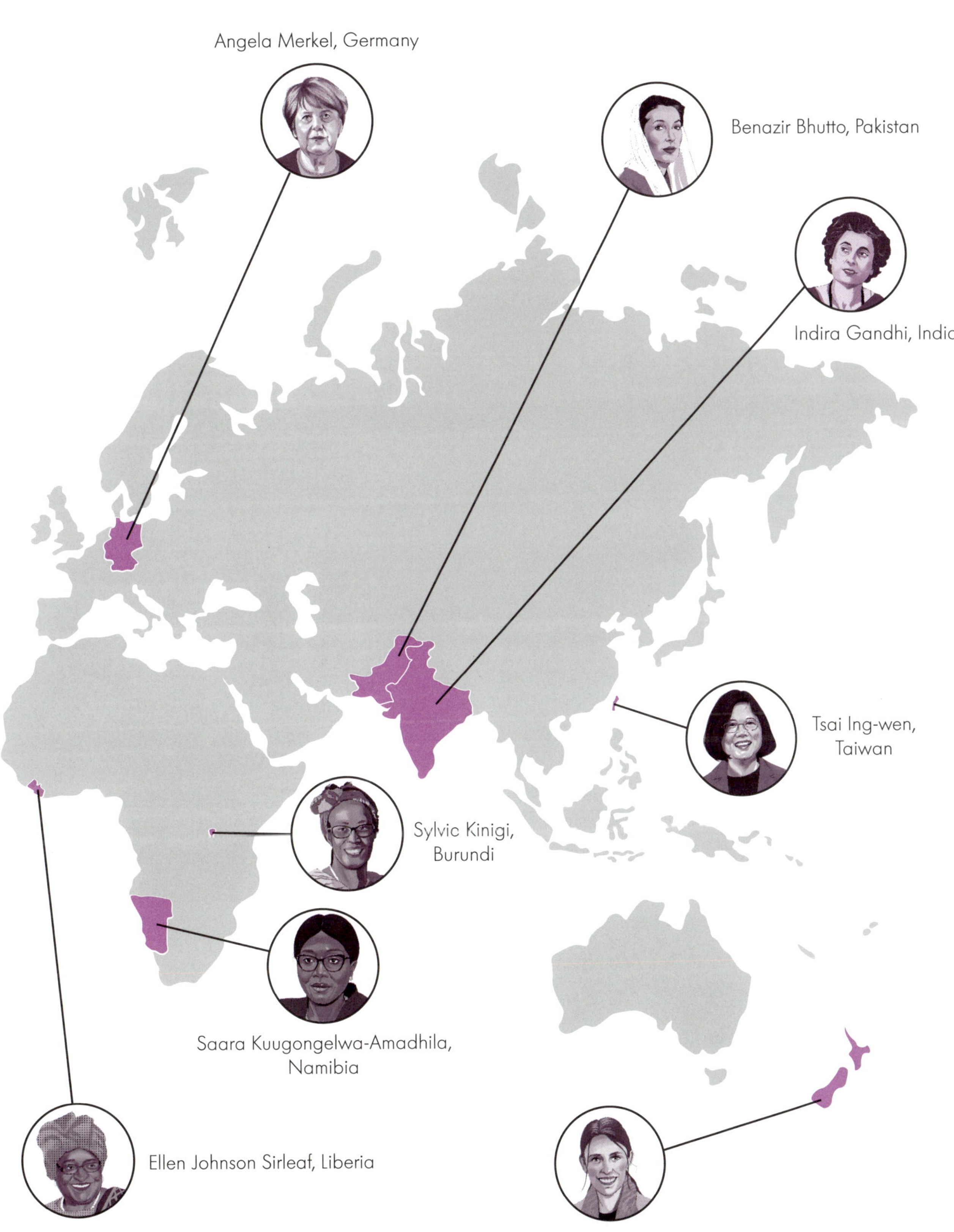
Angela Merkel, Germany
Benazir Bhutto, Pakistan
Indira Gandhi, India
Tsai Ing-wen,
Taiwan
Sylvic Kinigi,
Burundi
Saara Kuugongelwa-Amadhila,
Namibia
Ellen Johnson Sirleaf, Liberia
Jacinda Ardern, New Zealand

Introduction

There are more than two billion kids in the world today. These kids will grow up to do many amazing things: they'll develop new ideas and inventions that can help people and solve problems, they'll find cures for diseases, they'll achieve astonishing feats in sports and the arts, and so many wonderful things for their families and communities that will make our world a better place.

A very small group of kids will grow up to be the president or prime minister of their country.

Maybe *you* are one of them.

But let's step back for a minute. How does someone grow up to be the president or prime minister? Is there something special about these kids right from the moment they were born? What kinds of childhoods make someone want to become the leader of their country? What inspires them to lead? Can anyone really become a president or prime minister?

Here's a hard truth: our world is not an equal place. When we look at the world's leaders, we have a big problem. Not everyone gets a chance to lead.

Most countries in the world today, around 85 per cent, are led by a man (you can check out the United Nations "Women Political Leaders 2024" for more information). In fact, only about 40 per cent of countries have *ever* been led by a woman—which means that the majority of countries (60 per cent) have only been led by men. If we were to add up all the political leaders in all the countries around the world throughout all

of history, the total number of women leaders would be very (very!) tiny.

So, why is this a problem?

Political leaders govern by making many important decisions that affect all of us—things like what we learn at school, or whether we take care of our planet and animals, or what kinds of care we get when we're sick or need help. Through these decisions, political leaders shape our quality of life and how healthy, wealthy, safe, and happy we will be.

Research shows that when these important decisions are made by people with lots of different backgrounds and experiences and perspectives, *better decisions get made*—decisions that benefit more people.

Can we imagine a world where more of today's kids—and specifically, more girls—have an opportunity to become the president or prime minister if they want to? Can we create a future where leaders and governments look like the people they serve?

The answer is up to *you*.

Change doesn't happen on its own. It happens when people demand it. Books and movies are filled with amazing and inspiring stories about people throughout history who decided that better was possible, and they did something about it.

This book features girls who decided to aim for the top, becoming the prime minister or president in their country. They climbed over barriers, took courageous risks, and broke the molds for what political leaders usually look like. Was it hard? Yes. Did it make a difference? Absolutely! When girls and boys see women as political leaders, it sends an important message that women can, do, and should lead.

The girls in this book have many differences: they were born in different places and at different times and had different paths to eventually leading their countries. Some were born with great privilege; others faced significant barriers, even as

young kids. Several of them came from families of important men—and some became the first woman to take on the top leadership role. This book explores these origin stories: the childhoods of girls who became leaders and the early signs that they would one day change the world around them. We'll take a look at their first steps into politics and find out how their early experiences paved the way for their roles ahead.

These global leaders have different backgrounds, ideas, and opinions. They would likely disagree with one another on many important topics. But they share something essential in common: a belief that girls and women can lead, and a sense that they can create change around them.

Most of these women did not imagine that they would become president or prime minister when they were girls. As kids, they all had their own interests, hobbies, and passions—things that they cared about more than anything, perhaps the kinds of things that you care about, too. Sometimes, actions like standing up for a friend, standing up for someone that others are hurting, or speaking up about something that is wrong can end up being powerful and transformative acts of kindness.

You don't need to wait until you are prime minister or president or even a grown-up to incite change. You have the power right now to make things better for people around you.

You, too, can run the world like a girl.

Prime Minister Jacinda Ardern

NEW ZEALAND

New Zealand has been led by more than forty prime ministers. Just three have been women: Jenny Shipley, Helen Clark, and most recently, Jacinda Ardern. Of the more than five million people in New Zealand, what inspired Jacinda to lead her country?

Most people would say that Jacinda was born into a pretty normal family. She had an older sister named Louise and two parents, Laurell and David Ross Ardern. Her father was a police officer and everyone called him "Ross." Her mother, Laurell, stayed at home to raise Jacinda and her sister. At this time, it was common for fathers to work and make money to support their families, while mothers were expected to stay home and raise their children. That wasn't really what Laurell wanted to do, though.

PRIME MINISTER
Jacinda Ardern

- Born on July 26, 1980, in Hamilton, New Zealand
- Became involved in politics early in life, including serving as a **school trustee** and joining a political party as a teenager
- Served as the **prime minister of New Zealand** from 2017 to 2023
- Second woman in the world to **give birth while serving as a head of government** (after Pakistan's Benazir Bhutto)

Laurell was born on a dairy farm near Te Aroha—a rural community in the north island of New Zealand. New Zealand is an island country full of mountains and volcanos, with ocean-front beaches and lush forests. But Laurell didn't get to enjoy much of it. She was too busy working on the family farm. She, her sisters, and her brother would help their parents milk the cows and change the cows' bedding every single day. Laurell also worked in the town's post office. She eventually met Ross, and when she was twenty-one, she and Ross got married. Shortly after, they started having children. But she was still so young. Surely, she still had time to do all the things she wanted in life. Laurell wanted to go to university. She believed she could be a good mother and a good student at the same time. Then she could find the perfect job to help support her family and have some independence, too. But she didn't get the chance. With Ross's busy job and two young children, the family decided that Laurell would stay home to raise Jacinda and Louise.

When Jacinda was five years old, her dad got a new job in a small town called Murupara, nestled in the Kaingaroa Forest. There wasn't a whole lot to do there, and it was kind of a rough town. Moving away from family and friends was difficult, but Laurell found it particularly lonely. Many families didn't have enough money to pay for the things they needed. Whenever she walked around town with her family, Jacinda would see kids without shoes on. They were barefoot even when they went to school. And they rarely had anything to eat at lunchtime. Jacinda would look down at her food, and then down at her feet, and wonder why she had these things but other kids didn't. It was unfair and wrong. It filled her with a desire to help people, especially those in need.

Still, even if she couldn't do anything about it at the time, it didn't mean Jacinda forgot about it. Instead, she started paying closer attention to the world around her, keeping a look out for the ways that one person's life differed from someone else's. She didn't know the word for it yet, but what she was looking at was inequality. She even started to notice it in her own family. When Jacinda was eight years old, her dad got promoted. That meant they had to pack up and move again, no matter how anybody else felt about it. Her family purchased a small apple and nashi pear orchard from Laurell's parents. Living on a farm was a big responsibility, and everyone had to help.

At least, at first. As her dad's career progressed, he became involved in more serious crime investigations. He had to be away from home more often, leaving Laurell to look after the orchard and the girls. Laurell made most of Jacinda and Louise's clothing, and she taught her daughters to bake, cook, and make preserves.

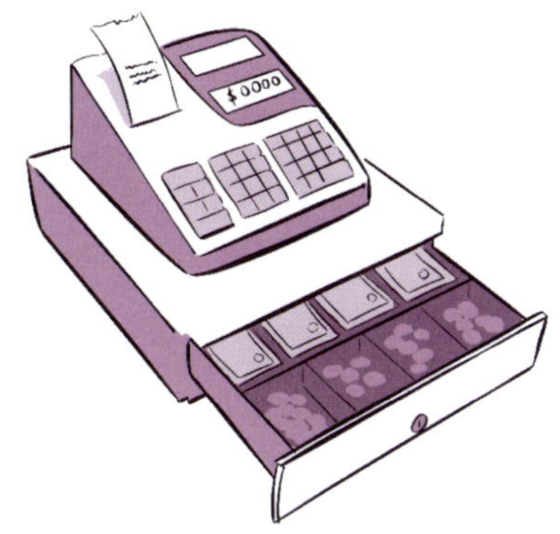

Through all of this, Jacinda was learning not only to watch out for inequality—she learned to listen for it, too. She listened closely to things her mother and sister told her about the world. She listened to kids at school vent about their problems. Listening to other people gave her time to develop her own ideas about things. She began to speak up more in class. So much so that she was elected to represent her classmates on the school board as a school trustee. She also worked after school as a cashier at a fish-and-chip shop. Sometimes, she would come home with less money than she earned. When her parents would ask her about it, she shared that when a customer was a few dollars short, Jacinda would offer to help pay.

Jacinda recognized that she could do things that would help people—from small acts of kindness to using her voice to call for big changes at school.

And she didn't stop there. When Jacinda was in high school, her aunt Marie encouraged her to get involved with politics. Marie was helping a member of parliament (MP) on his campaign for reelection—and Jacinda decided to help, too. She joined a political party, the New Zealand Labour Party, when she was seventeen years old, even though people must be eighteen years old to vote in New Zealand. Little did she know at the time that she would one day become the leader of the political party she had just joined.

After high school, Jacinda attended the University of Waikato, where she studied politics and public relations. During her degree, she spent some time abroad. She lived in New York City where she volunteered at a soup kitchen and joined a workers' rights campaign.

Jacinda graduated in 2001. She decided that pursuing a path in politics was the best way for her to help as many people as possible. She worked as a researcher for two New Zealand elected officials, including Prime Minister Helen Clark. Then she moved to the United Kingdom for a policy job under

British Prime Minister Tony Blair. At age twenty-seven, Jacinda was elected as president of the International Union of Socialist Youth—a role which brought her to several countries, including Jordan, Israel, Algeria, Hungary, and China.

In her late twenties, Jacinda decided to return home to New Zealand and run for public office herself. She ran as part of the Labour Party—the same party that she had volunteered for when she was in high school. Her goal was to become a member of parliament, which would mean that she could have a say in the laws that govern the whole country. She lost the election by 717 votes. But New Zealand has a way of electing representatives from party lists so that each party gets its fair share of seats in parliament. This is called proportional representation. The Labour Party got to add MPs who had high support from members of the party. Jacinda's party recognized her talents. They picked her to become an MP, and she became the youngest sitting member of parliament.

Jacinda's rise from here was rapid. In August 2017, she became the leader of her political party—just seven weeks before an election! What a busy time for Jacinda, as a new party leader and heading into a nationwide decision to choose a new government and prime minister. In October 2017, Jacinda led her party to create a new coalition and became New Zealand's fortieth prime minister.

In her first year as prime minister, Jacinda announced she was expecting a baby. It was almost unheard of for a prime minister to be pregnant and deliver a baby. Politicians, journalists, and even regular citizens peppered Jacinda with questions. "How will this work? Can a prime minister take a maternity leave?" Jacinda was clear about her plan: she would take six weeks off to give birth and be home with her child, and her partner, Clarke, would take a parental leave. That way, Jacinda could continue to lead as prime minister. This was an important shift from earlier generations, including her own mother's sacrifices to take care of Jacinda and her sister as children. Jacinda set an example for how women can lead, and the work of raising children can be shared more equally.

As her time as prime minister went on, people around the world came to admire how Jacinda led her country through difficult times. After a horrific Islamophobic attack on two mosques in the city of Christchurch, Jacinda mourned with the victims and their supporters and then introduced important gun reforms to keep people safe. During the COVID pandemic in 2020, Jacinda made hard decisions that kept more people safe. At times, she would share even the most important decisions through social media video messages recorded on her phone in a car or at a kitchen table. Quite different from most political messages delivered by someone in a suit behind a podium!

In Jacinda's words, "My hope for little girls and boys is that there is a future where they can make choices about how they raise their family and what sort of career they have, based on what they want and what makes them happy."

Prime Minister Benazir Bhutto

PAKISTAN

PRIME MINISTER
Benazir Bhutto

- Born in Karachi, Pakistan, on June 21, 1953, into a **famous and powerful political family**
- Elected as **prime minister of Pakistan** from 1988 to 1990 and from 1993 to 1996
- First woman elected to lead a **democratic government** in a Muslim-majority country
- **First woman head of government to give birth while in office** (with the second being New Zealand's Jacinda Ardern, three decades later)

The Bhutto family has been an important part of politics in Pakistan for generations. Long before she became prime minister, Benazir's father and grandfather had been politicians, too. This made the Bhuttos a political dynasty, where many members of the family held political roles. They are sometimes compared to the Kennedy family in the USA or the Nehru-Gandhi family in India.

Benazir was born into this wealthy political family in 1953. Her parents were Zulfikar Ali Bhutto and Nusrat Bhutto. Benazir was the oldest of four siblings. Her name means "incomparable and unique" (a lot to live up to!) but because she had a rosy color to her skin when she was born, her father Zulfikar called her "Pinkie."

Zulfikar had a big dream for his daughter: he wanted her to be the first girl in the Bhutto family to get an international education. In Pakistan's male-dominated culture, many girls did not have the same opportunities as their brothers to go to school. Zulfikar wanted to defy this trend. He told Benazir, "I ask only one thing of you: do well in your studies." As a little girl, Benazir enjoyed many advantages of growing up in a wealthy family. She got to learn many languages—English, Urdu, Persian, and Sindhi—and attended some of Pakistan's top schools.

Because her dad was so involved in politics, her parents were often away. As a kid, Benazir thought that she sometimes saw her dad in the newspaper more than she saw him at home! Her house was run by a staff team who would cook, clean, and look after the children. One night, before her parents were leaving for another long trip, Benazir's mom gave her a few rupees to help pay for food while they were away and told Benazir that because she was the oldest, she was in charge. Eight-year-old Benazir took this very seriously. She kept the money under her pillow that night and then talked to the head of the household staff—the majordomo—the next day about how they should spend it.

When Benazir's parents were home, the house became a busy place. Benazir would peek out the window when the fancy string lights were turned on and limousines would start arriving at their home, wondering who the important visitors would be. She liked to hear her father's stories about brave leaders in other countries, and hoped that the people coming to the fancy dinners would be the people from these stories.

When Benazir was ten, her parents decided to send her to boarding school. Not long after, war broke out between India and Pakistan. Benazir's father flew off to the United Nations to try to get other countries to help. Many of the kids at Benazir's school also had parents who were government or military officials, and they worried that the war might bring danger to the school. The teachers had the students practice what they would do if they were in danger. Before bed, Benazir would help tie another little girl's shoes on so that she would be prepared if they had to run in the middle of the night. Luckily, this never happened—but for Benazir, she learned that politics are important for keeping people safe.

When Benazir turned sixteen, her father's dream for her came true: she flew across the world to start at Harvard University in the United States. This was a big change for Benazir, being at a new school in a new country. For the first time in her life, nobody knew who she was or what family she came from. She was surprised to meet classmates at Harvard who knew little about

Pakistan at all, let alone the country's political leaders or her famous family. In fact, she lived at Harvard in a dorm room directly above a member of the Kennedy family, who was more famous than her in the United States! Benazir enjoyed both freedom and privacy for the first time in her life—but she also felt very lonely. America was a very different place from what she was used to. It was surprising to hear students openly criticizing their government without being afraid of getting hurt as a result. She was also not used to seeing boys and girls being treated equally at school and learning together in the same classrooms, as she had only attended all-girls' schools in Pakistan. When her American friends would go out for breakfast, they didn't know that as a Muslim, Benazir didn't eat bacon and pork.

One day in class, a Harvard professor was speaking about dictatorships and Pakistan's military policies. Benazir did not agree with what her professor was saying. She could feel her whole body heat up. Her heartbeat pounded in her ears. She realized that she was likely the only student in the room who had actually lived through a dictatorship. She stood up during the lecture and responded to her professor. Her hands and her voice were shaking in anger.

The other students were shocked. Word traveled around Harvard: Benazir was a powerful and charismatic speaker. She was finding her passion. She cared about politics, just like her father and grandfather, and she wanted to speak up for what's right.

It was good that Benazir learned this, because so much was changing back home in Pakistan—and although she didn't know it at the time, Benazir was going to play a big role. A movement was taking hold to bring democracy to Pakistan's government and organize opposition against the military dictatorship in power. While Benazir was away at Harvard, her father, Zulfikar, became the leader of the new Pakistan Peoples Party (PPP). Several of Benazir's other family members were very involved. Zulfikar, like his daughter, was a charismatic leader and played an important role in pushing for democratic elections to let citizens choose their political leaders. It worked—and Benazir's father was elected as the prime minister of Pakistan. Benazir graduated from Harvard, completed further studies at Oxford University in the United Kingdom, and then moved back home to Pakistan.

Benazir's return came at a highly chaotic time in Pakistan and for the Bhutto family. Zulfikar had been serving as prime minister for a few years and was reelected, but shortly after, he was overthrown in a military coup. Zulfikar was thrown in jail by his political opponents who had taken power. Nusrat and Benazir were invited to go visit Zulfikar in jail. They were horrified to learn that this was a final visit—the people who imprisoned Zulfikar had decided they were going to kill him. Zulfikar urged Benazir and Nusrat to leave Pakistan, worried that they, too, would face danger. Benazir refused. "We can't go. We'll never go. The generals will think they have won."

Zulfikar was right to be worried. After his death, Benazir and Nusrat were also imprisoned. Benazir was kept in solitary confinement. She spent her days and nights alone in a small cell, and she couldn't stand to swallow the food they gave her. Her body weakened, and her hair began to fall out as her health declined. But Benazir had well-connected friends from her time at Harvard and Oxford. Upon learning of her imprisonment, they negotiated with the Pakistani government to release Benazir.

Benazir believed in her father's vision for freedom and democracy in Pakistan and wanted to carry out his work. After her imprisonment, she got more involved in the Pakistan Peoples Party and was elected as leader of the party—just as her father had been before. She traveled the world to build connections and allies and spoke to big crowds in Pakistan about a different future for her country.

Benazir believed that getting married would increase her respectability among more traditional voters. Her mother, Nusrat, arranged her marriage to Asif Ali Zardari, and the wedding took place at the Bhutto family home. Many

described it as more of a political rally. Newspapers dubbed it the "People's Wedding" as over 200,000 people attended the wedding party in a nearby stadium! Not long after, Benazir announced she was having a baby.

The president of Pakistan at the time did not want Benazir to win the upcoming election. He scheduled the election for the same day that Benazir was due to give birth. His calculation was wrong, and the baby ended up arriving early—leaving Benazir with a newborn, messages of congratulations from media and well-wishers around the world, and five weeks to prepare for election day.

On election day, Benazir and the PPP won the most seats of any party in the election, and Benazir became the first woman prime minister of Pakistan, the first woman prime minister in a Muslim-majority country, and the youngest prime minister in the world. She was thirty-five years old.

Benazir served two terms as prime minister. She led Pakistan through a time when the country faced many challenges. It was not easy, but Benazir stayed focused on what got her involved in politics in the first place and the vision her father had for Pakistan.

In 2007, Benazir was speaking at a rally in Rawalpindi, Pakistan, and she and twenty-three other Pakistanis were killed by a bomb attack. This was shocking and heartbreaking for her supporters, and people mourned all across the country. Benazir had learned as a child that taking on political leadership roles can come with great personal risks—but for Benazir, just as for her father, those risks were worth it in the name of a shared vision of Pakistan.

Benazir once explained that,

> Leadership requires action: daring to take steps that are necessary but unpopular, challenging the status quo in order to reach a brighter future. To push for peace is ultimately personal

> sacrifice, for leadership is not easy. It is born of a passion, and it is a commitment. Leadership is a commitment to an idea, to a dream, and to a vision of what can be. And my dream is for my land and my people to cease fighting and allow our children to reach their full potential regardless of sex, status, or belief.

Benazir broke several glass ceilings as the first woman to lead Pakistan as prime minister, showing people that women, too, can be powerful drivers of change in their countries.

President Michelle Bachelet

CHILE

PRESIDENT
Michelle Bachelet

- Born in La Cisterna, Chile, on September 29, 1951
- Worked as a **doctor**
- **Speaks several languages** including Spanish, English, German, French, and Portuguese
- Served as the **president of Chile** from 2006 to 2010 and from 2014 to 2018
- Appointed as **United Nations High Commissioner for Human Rights** from 2018 to 2022

Chile is a beautiful country that, like so many others, has a complicated history. This long and narrow country sits along the western coast of South America and is the most southern country in the world, closer to the South Pole in Antarctica than any other country. Because the country is so long, it has remarkable natural diversity: warm to cold climates, and a range of vistas stretching between the beautiful Pacific Ocean coastline and the stunning Andes Mountains. But within all this beauty has also been violence.

In 1973, the people of Chile fell under the rule of a cruel dictator named Augusto Pinochet. It was a time of terror and hardship. Pinochet created laws that helped rich people make even more money, while poor people made less. Suffering was widespread. Anyone who spoke out against him could be arrested, or worse. Tens of thousands of people were imprisoned, and some were never seen again.

You might think that having lived through such difficult experiences, people would be too afraid to take risks. That no one would want to stand up for what was right. That they'd struggle to make big changes. But not too long after Pinochet's rule, Chile elected its first woman president: the remarkable Michelle Bachelet. A woman whose own father had been murdered during Pinochet's rule. How did this happen? How did this one girl in all of Chile's history rise to the top role of president?

Verónica Michelle (now known as Michelle) was born in 1951 in Chile's capital city, Santiago. She had a brother named Alberto who was five years older than her. Their parents were Ángela Margarita Jeria Gómez and Alberto Arturo Miguel Bachelet Martínez. Michelle's father was a pilot in the Chilean Air Force. As a young family, they frequently moved to various military bases and communities in Chile where her father was posted.

Being in a military family wasn't easy. Moving around a lot meant that Michelle and her brother had to always make new friends and sometimes learn new languages. When Michelle was twelve, her father was promoted to a new role in the Chilean Embassy in Washington, DC. Once again, the whole family had to pack up their lives and move. But this time was different. They weren't just moving to a different city in Chile—they were moving to an entirely new country! Most Americans only spoke English, not Spanish like they spoke in Chile. Michelle was used to adapting to new places and making new friends, but she had done all that in Spanish. How was she going to do that in Bethesda, Maryland, without knowing any English?

She and her brother had to learn English, while also learning all the usual subjects in school. It wasn't easy, but Michelle was determined to become fluent in English and be a good student. And she did.

Michelle's father later became a general in the Chilean Air Force, and they moved back to Chile. In both countries, Michelle worked hard in her studies and got involved in her school community. When she was in high school, she served as class president, played on the volleyball team, sang in choir, acted in school plays, and even played in a band that toured different school festivals. In 1969, she graduated high school near the top of her class. She wanted to study sociology or economics, but her father urged her to study medicine as a way to help people. She agreed. In 1970, Michelle began medical school at the University of Chile.

On September 11, 1973, Augusto Pinochet seized power of Chile through a military coup, taking over the democratically elected government. Pinochet proved to be a violent dictator. Immediately after seizing control of the country, he and his army began imprisoning and killing anyone who opposed him. It was an awful and tragic time for people in Chile, including Michelle and her family.

Michelle's father, Alberto, opposed the coup. Like others, he wanted Chile to have a government that was elected by the people of the country. Because of his opposition to the violent coup, Alberto was among the first people to be arrested and thrown in prison. It didn't matter that he was a high-ranking military official. In fact, it was his own colleagues from the Air Force who imprisoned him. They interrogated and tortured him for months. Alberto was later charged with treason, a crime meaning the betrayal of one's own country. Just six months after the coup, Alberto died in a jail in Santiago where he was being tortured.

It was an unthinkably sad loss for Michelle and her family—and the nightmare wasn't over yet. About a year after her father's death, Michelle and her mother Ángela were in their apartment when they heard a loud knock at the door. Michelle slowly got up from her seat to see who it was, but before she could, the lock clicked, and the door opened to reveal two men in uniform. Members of Pinochet's secret police. There was nothing Michelle and her mother could do to fight as the men blindfolded them and forced them out of their apartment. The women were driven to a secret detention center and then separated. Michelle and her mother were interrogated and tortured. Thankfully, they both survived.

Through the help of a humanitarian diplomat, Michelle was able to escape in exile to Australia and then to East Germany. She continued her medical studies and met another Chilean exile, an architect named Jorge Leopoldo Dávalos Cartes. They married, and a year later, Michelle gave birth to a son, Jorge Alberto Sebastián.

In 1979, Michelle got approval to return home to Chile. When she got home, she learned that her medical studies from East Germany would not be recognized. She had to start her education all over again, but this did not stop Michelle from pursuing her goal. Four years later, she graduated as a physician and surgeon, but her request to work in the areas she wanted was denied "on political grounds."

Michelle specialized in children's health. She got a job working for an organization that helped children whose parents were missing or had been tortured. By this time, Michelle had three children of her own. She was busy with family and work. After everything that the military government in Chile had taken from her, it would have been easy to stay angry and stay out of politics. Michelle did the opposite.

After her return from exile, Michelle got involved in efforts to restore democracy to Chile. She joined a political party and ran for mayor of Las Condes, a suburb of Santiago. Michelle finished fourth, receiving only 2.35 per cent of the vote. This did not dissuade her.

By the 1990s, Pinochet had been arrested for human rights violations. Democracy had returned to Chile, and citizens had elected a new president, Ricardo Lagos. He saw Michelle's talents and appointed her to the important role of improving the healthcare system in Chile. She then became the first woman minister of national defense. One of her most important tasks was to encourage reconciliation between the military and victims of the Pinochet dictatorship. Michelle knew all too well how badly this reconciliation was needed.

Michelle became well-known for her work in these roles. Many people respected her, both in the government and outside of it, especially after she led a rescue mission following a flood in Santiago in 2002. Newspapers ran photos of her in a cloak and cap, leading a crew of rescuers without fear. People were moved and impressed by her efforts. There was an election coming up, and people kept asking Michelle to run for president. She reflected on what she wanted to see happen in Chile and decided that she wanted to step up. In 2005, she was elected as the leader of the Socialist Party. In 2006, she led her party to a majority victory and became the first (and to date, only) woman president of Chile. Michelle was also the first woman in all of Latin America to reach presidency through direct election without being the wife of a previous political leader.

Immediately after her election as president, Michelle announced that she would be appointing Chile's first gender-balanced cabinet—meaning the group of ministers in charge of important areas like healthcare and the economy would be made up of 50 per cent men and 50 per cent women.

Michelle served two terms as president. For most world leaders, reaching this top role would be the peak of a career—but not for Michelle. In 2018, Michelle was appointed to a global role as the United Nations high commissioner for human rights. She has been ranked by *Forbes* magazine as one of the most powerful women in the world.

In Michelle's words, "It was said that Chile was not ready to vote for a woman, it was traditionally a sexist country. In the end, the reverse happened: the fact of being a woman became a symbol of the process of cultural change the country was undergoing." Michelle survived one of Chile's most violent and difficult periods. Despite enduring great losses and facing huge challenges, she remained strong in her resolve to help other people. Her experiences fueled her to become a powerful champion of human rights in Chile and around world.

Prime Minister Kim Campbell

CANADA

PRIME MINISTER
Kim Campbell

- Born in Port Alberni, Canada, on March 10, 1947
- Became the first woman **student council president** in her high school
- Served as an **elected official** within her province and country
- Served as **prime minister of Canada** in 1993, the only woman in Canada who has held this role to date

Which country has the longest coastline in the world? Canada! A vast territory stretching between the Pacific, Atlantic, and Arctic oceans, Canada is home to the rugged Rocky Mountains, sprawling prairies, beautiful forests, and majestic lakes. It is known as a "mosaic" because of the diversity of people who live in Canada. Today, almost two hundred different languages are spoken! People from all over the world have chosen to move to Canada, retaining their culture and faith and traditions. This is an ambition, but unfortunately, it has not always been everyone's experience. There is much work still to be done: meaningful reconciliation with Indigenous Peoples and striving to be a welcoming and safe place with opportunities for everyone.

Canadians celebrate living in an inclusive place—and yet, Canada's political leaders have not reflected this diversity. To date, only one woman has ever served as prime minister—and that was just for 132 days. Canada's provinces and territories have also been led by very few women (you can read about them in *Govern Like a Girl*, the Canadian edition!).

So, who was the only Canadian girl who grew up to become prime minister? Her story begins in British Columbia, where you can find ancient trees and the Rocky Mountains. And her name wasn't Kim Campbell—at least, not yet.

George Campbell and Lissa Cook met during World War II when George was stationed at Port Alberni in the province of British Columbia. The young couple married in 1944, just months before George was sent overseas. Four months later, he returned to Lissa and a new three-month-old daughter, Alix. Shortly after, the couple welcomed a second girl: Avril Phaedra Douglas Campbell.

Avril was a spunky kid. When she was about ten years old, her parents moved to Vancouver. Avril was cast as a kid reporter on the show *Junior Television Club* hosted by the Canadian Broadcasting Corporation (CBC). Avril was a star! She loved using her voice to talk about important things.

While Alix and Avril were growing up in Vancouver, their parents drifted apart. They sent the girls away to a boarding school in Victoria. Avril excelled at her new school. One of her teachers claimed she was the only student during her entire career to get every question right on an IQ test. However, when Avril was twelve years old, she and her sister got some very bad news: their mother had left suddenly and moved to Europe, without saying a word to her daughters. Avril and her sister couldn't believe it. How could this happen? The girls wanted to go home to be with their father, but he felt it was best for them to finish the school year. It was hard, but Avril kept up with her studies and completed the year—but she decided to change her name from the one given to her by her mother. From this point forward, she was known as Kim Campbell, and she was driven to succeed. Kim wasn't going to let this hard experience define her.

In high school, Kim was a very hard worker. She was a top student. She liked to play music and write poetry. She found that the more she practiced something, like music, the better she could do it. She also liked to lead, and every time an opportunity came up, Kim went for it. She ran for student council president—and became the first girl ever at her school to win! Kim learned something really important about herself through this experience:

> When I was in high school, I realized that I could move people when I spoke. I realized that this carries with it a huge moral responsibility. When you have the ability to connect with people, you can do great harm as well as great good with it. And I always wanted to do good.

Even though she had done so many activities as a teen, Kim wasn't sure what she wanted to do for the rest of her life. She liked playing music, writing, and being part of a team that worked to make the school community better—how could she turn that into a job? There was a lot of pressure to decide on her life path. It would shape not just her career but also the type of person she would become and who did she want to be? She wasn't totally sure yet. She needed to learn more about herself first. So, Kim completed an undergraduate degree in political science at the University of British Columbia—but she still didn't know what she wanted to do. She went on to earn a master's degree and a PhD, then taught courses at university. She completed a law degree, too. And finally, she knew: Kim learned that she had a superpower to connect with people when she spoke. She decided to run in an election. She wanted to use her voice to help other people.

Kim was elected to the Vancouver school board, making important decisions about education in her community. She quickly rose to a leadership role, becoming the chair of the board—a big honor! Others saw how effective Kim was at leading and encouraged her to run for a larger role. Kim decided to run in a provincial election so she could make decisions that would help everyone in British Columbia, not just her city.

Kim's first run in a provincial election wasn't successful, but she wasn't deterred. The leader of her party stepped down, so Kim decided to take a very big step: she decided to run for party leader. She disagreed with the former leader on a few important issues, including women's rights. Kim wanted to stand up for women.

Leadership races end at a big party called a "convention," where the leader is chosen by members of the party. Kim was so nervous. When it was her turn to speak, she went up on stage and spoke about all of the things that mattered most to her and the kinds of changes she wanted to see in her party and province. She spoke so well that many people said it was the best speech of the convention! But when the winner was announced, one of the men running won. Kim came last in the group—but just like when she was a kid, she didn't let this setback stop her. She ran again in the next provincial election. This time, she won.

This victory began Kim's rapid rise in Canadian politics. People saw Kim leading and using her voice for good and encouraged her to take another big step. What if she could help make decisions for her entire country, not just her province? This sounded pretty exciting to Kim. After three years of serving the province of British Columbia, Kim ran in a federal election and won her seat. She was now part of the government of Canada. She served as a provincial elected official for three years and then decided to run for federal politics. In 1988, Kim was elected as a member of parliament.

Shortly after Kim was elected, she received a phone call from the prime minister, Brian Mulroney. How exciting! Why was the prime minister calling her? The prime minister asked if she could meet with him at seven o'clock. Right away, she booked a plane ticket to travel from Vancouver to Ottawa. When she arrived, she and her husband went out for dinner. While they were eating, she got another phone call. It was the prime minister. He asked, "Where are you?!" Kim was horrified. She had thought he wanted to meet with her at 7:00 a.m. the next morning, not 7:00 p.m. that night! The prime minister of Canada was waiting to meet with her and Kim hadn't shown up! "We should be having this conversation in person," he said, "but I'd like to name you as a minister in my cabinet." Wow! What a huge honor to get to make important decisions and use her voice for good. Kim was delighted. She ended up serving in a few different minister roles, being responsible for things like the justice system, and was often the first woman ever to be in those important jobs.

In February 1993, the prime minister announced that he was retiring from politics. That meant the party had to choose a new leader. Because the Progressive Conservative Party was in government, the new leader of Kim's party would automatically become prime minister. It was a big task: whoever would become the prime minister would also have to lead their party almost immediately in an election, and the party wasn't as popular as it used to be.

Many people asked Kim to run. They respected the work that she had done so far. Plus, people knew about Kim's superpower as a great public speaker. The party needed a dynamic new leader, and she seemed perfect for the role. But the country had never had a woman prime minister. Would people vote for a party led by a woman? Could people imagine having a woman as their prime minister? Some people worried that having a woman leader might hurt the party in the election.

Kim was up for the challenge. She decided to run. Just like when she ran in a provincial leadership race, the other people running were all men. Kim traveled across the country to speak to party members—the people who would be voting for the new leader. By the end of the race, she had built a big team of supporters. Once again, she found herself at a leadership convention, nervous to find out the results. The large room echoed with the eager voices of the crowd, but everyone fell silent when Kim walked on stage as the song "A New Sensation" played over the speakers. She made a speech about why she wanted to lead the party and Canada. She talked about building trust, a strong economy, and chances for people to participate in decisions that affect them. After, the votes were counted, and Kim won! The crowd chanted her name as Kim Campbell became the nineteenth prime minister of Canada on June 25, 1993.

There was no time to rest after winning the leadership race. The country was heading into an election and as a new leader, Kim had to convince Canadians that she was up to the job of continuing to be their prime minister. She again traveled across the country campaigning—making speeches to try to convince people to vote for her party—while also doing the work of being the prime minister. She changed how her cabinet of top leaders was organized and made decision-making more efficient. Kim was busy seven days a week. What a whirlwind!

During the election campaign, there were many challenges. Kim's party had been in power for almost a decade, and many Canadians were not happy with things the party had done. The media and voters asked Kim tough questions about whether she was up for the job, because they had never seen a woman be prime minister before.

On election night, the results were clear: Kim and her party had lost. After just 132 days as prime minister, Kim's political career came to an end.

Kim was a determined kid. She worked hard and wasn't afraid to use her voice and speak up about things that mattered to her. To date, Kim remains the first and only woman to serve as prime minister of Canada. In her words, "I'd be prouder still to say I was Canada's tenth woman prime minister."

Canada is a diverse country—a mosaic—but this has not yet extended into politics. Most leadership roles are still held by white men. As Kim knows, in Canada there is still a long way to go.

President Ellen Johnson Sirleaf

LIBERIA

PRESIDENT

Ellen Johnson Sirleaf

- Born in Monrovia, Liberia, in 1938
- Married at age seventeen and had four sons; **stayed home to raise children until pursuing her education later in life**
- Served as **president** of Liberia from 2006 to 2018
- **First elected woman head of state** in Africa
- Won the **Nobel Peace Prize** in 2011

Oftentimes, the story of a country's leader is like a mini version of the story of the country itself. The changes and challenges the leader experiences reflect the changes and challenges of the whole nation. No story is more fitting than Ellen Johnson Sirleaf's, the first woman president of Liberia.

Liberia is a country in western Africa with a coastline along the North Atlantic Ocean. While people have lived in the area for hundreds of thousands of years, Liberia as a nation began in the 1800s. Previously enslaved African Americans or those who had been born free began migrating to Africa in the hopes of creating a better life than they could have in the United States. Over time, they developed the Republic of Liberia and declared independence in 1847. It was the first African republic to proclaim independence and one of only two African nations (along with Ethiopia) to remain independent during the "scramble for Africa," when European countries sought to colonize all of the continent. Today, Liberia is home to more than 5.5 million people. The official language is English, with more than twenty other Indigenous languages also spoken.

Like the country she grew up to lead, Ellen has a long and winding life story, one that is influenced by global history and diverse cultures. Ellen's grandmother, Juah Sarwee, was a farmer and market worker in Greenville, Liberia, in the early 1900s. Greenville was a major port city, with many ships coming in to do trade. At the time, Germany was one of Liberia's main trading partners, and Liberia's markets were full of Germans seeking to export Liberia's natural resources, like coffee and palm oil. Juah met and fell in love with a German trader. She became pregnant and gave birth to a daughter, Martha. They might have been a happy family of three, but things did not work out that way. At the start of World War I, Liberia declared war on Germany and forced all the Germans to leave the country to build favor with the United States. Martha's father left, never to be heard from again.

Martha looked quite different from the other children in her village. White settlers saw her as a white child with an illiterate, poor, and struggling Black mother and offered to take them in. These people treated Martha as a slave, denying her a room or bed of her own. Her days were filled with chores, and in the evening, she would sleep under the table with the family's animals. A wealthy woman named Cecilia Dunbar heard about the mistreatment of a young "white" girl and offered a payment to take her in as an adopted child. The payment was accepted, and Martha became the only child of a wealthy family with access to an excellent education.

Years later, Martha was in her backyard when a tall, stylish man walked by. He was struck by Martha's beauty. He was much older than Martha. They spoke briefly and then he went on his way. But then he came back to have another conversation with Martha. It happened again and again. Over time, Martha realized he was romantically interested in her. His name was Jahmale Carney Johnson. His father was a Gola chief, meaning he was a leader within an important tribe. Jahmale worked as a lawyer and, later on, entered politics, becoming the first Indigenous person to be elected to the national legislature in Liberia. After countless meetings with Martha, Jahmale came to the house and proposed to Martha, also seeking permission from Cecilia. Both women saw how charming and intelligent Jahmale was and immediately said yes. The couple got married, settled into a new house, and began having children.

Born in 1938, Ellen was their youngest daughter. Looking back on her childhood, Ellen fondly remembers all the happy times when she got to spend time with her grandmothers and traveled to her father's home village, where she learned to swim and fish in the Kpo River. It was a nice childhood, but not everything was easy. Her father was often away from home for work. In Jahmale's absence, Martha led the household. She decided to become a traveling pastor in the Presbyterian Church. This meant that Ellen and her three siblings often had to join her on the religious trips, traveling by foot or canoe to small villages for Sunday services.

When Ellen was seven, she and her siblings went with their mother to a small town called Careysburg. Martha asked Ellen to give a recitation at the church on Sunday morning. Ellen was terrified at the thought. She spent Saturday afternoon trying to memorize her lines for what would be her first public speaking experience. The next morning, Ellen was called in front of the congregation. Once on stage, she couldn't remember a single word of her lines! Ellen started to cry, and the congregation clapped in kindness as Ellen went back to sit down with her mother. Martha tried to console Ellen, saying, "These things happen!" But Ellen silently vowed to herself that she would never fail in public speaking again.

When Ellen was in high school, she went to the movies with friends. There, she met a man much older than her named James but called "Doc." They started to date. Doc was a jealous type, and Ellen's parents warned her about getting too close to this older man. But Ellen was in love. At age seventeen, she finished high school and married Doc. While some of her friends were heading off to college, Ellen was home with her first son, soon followed by three more. Doc took a job with the Ministry of Agriculture, leaving Ellen home to raise the boys basically all on her own.

Ellen wasn't happy. Her childhood had ended so suddenly, and her life was now filled with caring for her own children. She thought of how her mother Martha had defied the odds and avoided a life in poverty. Ellen didn't want to settle for the life she had. She told herself, "This can't be the end for me. I have to do something."

Doc won a scholarship to complete a master's degree in the United States, and Ellen jumped at the chance to move. This was it—the opportunity she had been waiting for. She applied to study business in the United States. But what would happen to her young boys? She asked her family to care for them, as extended families often share the work of raising children in African cultures. Although it was hard to leave her children, Ellen was excited for her new adventure: pursuing an education in America.

Doc and Ellen rented an apartment and they both began their studies. Unfortunately, now that they were together all the time in a small apartment and in a new, unfamiliar country, problems began to emerge in their relationship. Doc became jealous of anyone who talked to Ellen, and he developed a serious drinking problem. He was abusive and controlling. Ellen took a job at a department store to help pay the bills. Doc was embarrassed that his wife needed to work. One day, he came to Ellen's work and screamed at her in front of her coworkers, demanding she go home. It was humiliating for Ellen. She wasn't happy—but she clung to her view that better was always possible for her. She knew she needed to make a change. She finished her education, graduating from Harvard, and returned home to Liberia to reunite with her children and begin working—and, she divorced Doc.

Now that she had a solid education and was free of Doc, Ellen could finally take control of her own life. She began working as an administrator for a politician. Because of her strong training in economics, she was offered the position of assistant minister of finance. Over time, Ellen took on increasingly more important roles, including working for the World Bank and Citibank, two of the biggest international banks. She was appointed as a director for a United Nations development

program. She ran for office for the first time in 1985 and won—but refused to accept her seat due to the unfair and undemocratic way the election was conducted.

This wasn't the first time she had criticized the government and the way they ran the country. In fact, she had become famous for making "bombshell" statements about how the government and big corporations were harming Liberia. Many people in power didn't like the things she said. At one point, she even had to flee the country to keep herself safe. But this time, she didn't get a chance to flee—she was arrested and sentenced to prison. Eventually, she was released and had to leave the country once again.

This wasn't the end of the difficulties for Ellen or for Liberia. The country had been dealing with years of civil war, which is when people of different groups in the same country fight each other. Many people were killed. Ellen, and others like her, were uncertain if they could ever make Liberia the free and democratic nation they wanted it to be. But Ellen wasn't about to stop trying. In 2003, the second Liberian Civil War came to an end, and Ellen was appointed to a leadership role in the new transitional government. Later that year, she ran for president in the general election and won, becoming the president of Liberia and the first woman to be elected to lead any African country. And then she did it all again in 2011.

In Ellen's words, "If your dreams do not scare you, they are not big enough. The size of your dreams must always exceed your current capacity to achieve them." Ellen came from a family of women who believed that they could rise up from the challenges they faced. Ellen lived this belief, too—and in doing so, she was able to create big changes in her country.

Prime Minister Indira Gandhi

INDIA

PRIME MINISTER
Indira Gandhi

- Born in Allahabad, Uttar Pradesh, India, on November 19, 1917
- Served as **prime minister of India for fifteen years**, from 1966 to 1977 and again from 1980 to 1984
- **Daughter of the first prime minister of India**, and **mother of the prime minister who succeeded her in office**
- **Only woman prime minister of India** to date
- **Second-longest serving Indian prime minister**, after her father

India is considered one of the world's oldest countries, with human civilization dating back tens of thousands of years. Ancient Indian societies had many notable women rulers and important government figures. In modern society, however, women leaders are less common. In recent years, India has had two woman presidents: Pratibha Patil (elected in 2007) and Droupadi Murmu (elected in 2022). But way before them, there was Indira Gandhi. In 1966, Indira became one of the first women to be elected as prime minister in the world.

How did she do it? Let's start at the beginning.

Kamala Kaul was born in 1899 in Delhi, India. She was the oldest of four children. When she was a teenager, her parents arranged her marriage to twenty-seven-year-old Jawaharlal Nehru. Jawaharlal was a lawyer from an important political family. Arranged marriages were common at this time but sometimes came with a cost: for many girls, this marked the end of their opportunity to go to school or pursue their own dreams. Kamala was seventeen when she got married. One year later, she gave birth to a baby girl named Indira.

Indira's father, Jawaharlal, was a leader in India's independence movement. At the time, much of the country was governed by Queen Victoria under a colonial system known as the British Raj. This meant that Indians did not have control over their own decisions or future for their country. They could not vote for their leaders or have any say in the country's future. The British rule was undemocratic and exploitative. The British Raj also encouraged fighting among different religious groups—if the Indian people were divided, they wouldn't unite together to get rid of British rule. Jawaharlal wanted India to achieve independence from Britain. Even though Indira's family was wealthy and didn't suffer as much as other people, they did not want their fellow Indians to suffer. Kamala shared Jawaharlal's commitment to India's independence. She didn't want to follow tradition and become a housewife. She wanted to help in the movement.

When Indira was just four years old, her father was supposed to give a major speech to a crowd of supporters. But the authorities found out about it. They knew how powerful his words could be, so they arrested him. After Jawaharlal was arrested, Indira's mother Kamala went to the event instead and delivered the speech. Kamala was popular among supporters of Indian independence and she organized many women's groups. Meanwhile, Jawaharlal ended up being imprisoned eight times, spending more than nine years in prison during Indira's childhood.

Because of this, Indira did not have a happy childhood. She grew up in her father's large family estate in Allahabad (today known as Prayagraj). The house was called Anand Bhavan and had forty-two rooms, including its own library. People in the independence movement would often meet at her house to plan protests and other events. It should have been very exciting to live in such luxury, surrounded by political leaders doing important work. And yet, it wasn't. Sometimes, it was even scary. Indira could hear the adults talking downstairs, and suddenly the police would arrive, sometimes arresting the adults—including her father.

Indira rarely saw her father as he was always either away or in prison. Her mother Kamala gave birth to a baby boy when Indira was seven, but tragically, the baby passed away a few days later. Then Kamala became very sick with tuberculosis and had to travel away for medical treatment. Without her parents, Indira struggled to connect to people. She was often alone. Although she some-

times went to girls' schools, she was mostly taught by tutors at home. As such, Indira grew up introverted and shy. For her, Anand Bhavan was a lonely place.

While Indira's father was in prison, he would send her letters. Even if he couldn't be at home with her, he wanted to teach her all about the history of the world and the relationships between different countries or cultures. In other letters, he urged Indira to think critically about injustices in the world around her. Ten-year-old Indira got so excited when letters arrived. She missed her father so much, and seeing "My dear Indira" written at the top, and "Your loving father" scrawled at the bottom made Indira feel closer to her dad. His words were so inspiring. He talked to her about being brave, telling the truth, and having courage when it comes to the things that matter most.

When Indira was thirteen, she and her mother attended an independence protest in Allahabad. It was a very hot day. Bodies jostled close together under the heat of the bright sun. To Indira, the voice of the speaker seemed to be coming from far away. She turned to her mother and saw the sweat dripping from her face. Indira was sweating too, and as she wiped the moisture from her eyes, her mother began to sway. The next thing Indira knew, her mother was on the ground. Her eyes fluttered. What was Indira to do? Suddenly, a young man was at her side, helping her mother sit up. Indira had seen the man before: he was Feroze Gandhi, a member of the independence movement. Later that year, she heard that Feroze had been put in prison. Still, he was able to stay close with the family. They exchanged letters, and he came to visit the family home once. When Indira was sixteen, Feroze asked Indira if she would marry him. Indira and her mother rejected the proposal, saying that Indira was still too young to marry.

Over time, Kamala's health worsened. Indira traveled with her to Germany for special treatment. They discussed Indira's future education. They were both so hopeful about the possibilities to come, but sadly, Kamala became more and more ill, and eventually passed away.

It was such a sad time for Indira. Her father was in prison. Her mother was gone. She felt lost—and she needed a new direction. She decided to move away to attend Somerville College, a well-known women's college at Oxford University in the United Kingdom. For the first time in her life, she was in an entirely new place and surrounded by people her own age. She joined a debating group that had been founded by other Indian students and started making friends. She liked learning about history and politics—it reminded her so much of the letters her father had written her when she was a child. But it wasn't all fun. Indira had to take courses in Latin and she hated it. She struggled so much that she had to repeat a few of her exams. She also ran into a familiar face—Feroze was also studying in the United Kingdom! Indira and Feroze started spending a lot of time together. The same similar interests that brought them together on that hot day in Allahabad meant they had lots to talk about. Indira and Feroze grew close to one another. In 1942, when Indira was twenty-four years old, she and Feroze got married. Over the next four years, the couple had two sons.

While Indira's childhood had often been hard and lonely, her adulthood brought exciting new possibilities and challenges. After generations of struggle for independence, India began to change before Indira's eyes. World War II had just ended, and Britain was no longer a wealthy empire like they used to be. They couldn't afford to keep control over their colonies, including India. Meanwhile, the Indian people had already created their own governments right under the noses of the British. Mahatma Gandhi, famous for his peaceful protests, led the Quit India Movement to urge the British to leave India. Mahatma and many others were imprisoned, including Indira—but the time for change had finally come. In August 1947, India achieved independence. Indira's father, Jawaharlal, had been a strong and powerful force in the independence movement. People already saw him as a leader—and with India's independence, Indira's father became the first prime minister. Her husband, Feroze, was also an elected official.

Politics had been a part of Indira's whole life, but she never imagined herself as a politician. Sometimes, people would ask her to get involved, and she would always say no. She was busy campaigning for her father or her husband, and her children were still so young. She was also busy helping in refugee camps or expanding schools and education. She liked what she was doing, and she'd witnessed what it meant to have a life in politics. But people kept asking her to get more involved and take on leadership roles. She tried to stay in the background, but before she knew it, she was nominated to be president of her party. She took on several important roles, and people could see that she was a strong and capable leader.

In 1964, Jawaharlal died suddenly from a heart attack. For the country and for Indira, this came as a shock. Indira was devastated. She'd already lost her mother, and now her father as well. It became even more difficult because this loss also brought a period of change in the political leadership of her country. Within a few months, Indira could see that her father's vision for their country was being threatened. A new leader who shared Jawaharlal's commitment was needed. The senior men in the party thought that Indira would be the best choice to run for two reasons: she was already well-known because of her name and her father, and because they assumed that as a younger woman, she would be easy to control. After some protest, Indira agreed to serve. She was elected with a lot of support, becoming the first woman prime minister in India. When she came out of parliament, the crowd chanted, "Long live the red rose," in reference to her father's symbol.

At first, some people saw Indira as weak. There had never been a woman as prime minister before. The men who convinced her to run told her that she owed her role to them for having encouraged her to run. Indira often thought of the letters from her father. He told her to be brave and courageous. She quickly showed her opponents just how much they were underestimating her. Over her first decade as prime minister, she became known internationally as a strong, powerful, and decisive leader. She led her party through several elections. She is the second-longest serving prime minister in India's history, second only to her father. She served as prime minister until her death in 1984.

In Indira's words, "Even if I died in the service of my country, I would be proud of it." As a child, she saw up close the kind of sacrifice that it takes to be a political leader. It wasn't a path she initially imagined for herself, but when she believed her country needed her, she was willing to follow in the footsteps of her father and serve. Indira lived at a critical time in India's history, and she holds an important place in that history for her contributions, her resolve, and her strength as a leader.

President Vigdís Finnbogadóttir

ICELAND

PRESIDENT
Vigdís Finnbogadóttir

- Born in Reykjavík, Iceland, on April 15, 1930
- Worked in **theater and taught French lessons on television**
- Served as **president of Iceland** from 1980 to 1996
- **First woman in the world to be democratically elected as president**, and the **longest-serving woman head of state** in any country

Iceland is a small, northern island country, home to just 400,000 residents. Even though it's small, the country has done big things! Iceland is often celebrated as one of the most egalitarian nations on earth—meaning that all people are treated equally and have access to the same opportunities. Icelandic women made strides toward gender equality much earlier than most countries, sometimes several decades before other governments even began to think about making these changes.

In 1850, daughters in Iceland gained the same rights of sons to inherit things from their parents. In 1882, widows and wealthy single women gained the right to vote for the mayors of their cities and towns. Not too long after, girls and young women got more opportunities for education when the first women's colleges were founded. By the early 1900s, all women in Iceland could vote, and the first women were elected to office. Icelanders took big steps toward gender equality ahead of most of the world—including in 1980, when they elected the world's first woman president, Vigdís Finnbogadóttir.

Vigdís was born in Reykjavík, the capital of and the largest city in Iceland. Reykjavík was a close-knit community. The harsh weather and extreme climates meant that people had to rely on each other. The city had a busy harbor, with ships bringing in and sending out goods to other countries. Because the city is so far north, during the winter, the sun is only out for about four hours per day! People have to work together to get through the coldest and darkest months.

Vigdís's family was well-connected and worked hard to help others in the community. Her father, Finnbogi Rútur Thorvaldsson, was an engineer who

designed shipping ports, which were very important in Iceland! He also taught engineering at the University of Iceland. Vigdís's mother, Sigrídur Eiríksdóttir, was a nurse. Sigrídur also served as the chairperson for the Icelandic Nurses Association for more than thirty-five years. This meant that when Vigdís was a kid, her mom was on the phone a lot. People would call their house if they needed a nurse. Her mom would then call a nurse, and they would head out on their bicycle to help the patient. Vigdís's little brother, Thorvaldur, would complain that their mom was on the phone too much, so Vigdís started helping her mom handle all the calls, keeping track of the requests for nurses. Because of this work, Vigdís knew a lot about her community—including every single doctor and nurse in Reykjavík by name!

Vigdís's grandparents were also a big part of her life. Her grandmother was one of the first women to seek a divorce in Iceland and worked cleaning floors at the library to take care of her young children. When the men who gathered at the library started talking to her, they realized how smart she was and asked her to join their discussions. Vigdís's grandmother would always encourage the girls in the family to pay attention to the world around them and never be afraid to speak up.

When Vigdís was in elementary school, many countries were fighting in World War II. This was a very scary time for many people, including kids in Iceland. At Vigdís's school, the kids would have practice drills for what to do if their school was being attacked. The kids had to hide under tables covered in heavy rugs. Vigdís would always go find her little brother, Thorvaldur, so they could hide together. She wanted to make sure that he wasn't too scared.

By the time Vigdís was a teenager, the war was over. Vigdís was able to focus on different things: her friends, her love of art and drama, and going to dances with her friends. But her parents were very strict. One night, there was a dance that Vigdís wanted to attend but her parents said she wasn't allowed to go. She snuck out anyway to go with her friends. When she got to the dance, guess who was there? Her dad, who sometimes taught night courses! He didn't see her, but she went home as quickly as she could.

As a teenager, Vigdís felt embarrassed about her own looks. Her Irish descent meant that she had rosy skin and lots of freckles. She begged her parents for money to purchase anti-freckle cream, which she put on diligently every night before bed. One summer day, she went outside, and the hot sun brought out more freckles than she'd ever seen before. She hated her freckles until she saw the movie *The Wizard of Oz*. The main character, Dorothy, also had lots of freckles, and Vigdís thought she looked so beautiful! What a relief. Vigdís learned to love her own look—and she learned what a powerful influence people on television and theater can have on those who watch their performances.

This was a big lesson for Vigdís because she loved the arts. Her parents had always encouraged her to pursue an education in the areas she loved. When she'd make paper dolls as a kid and act out plays with them, her parents welcomed her to set up her paper figures all around their house. So, Vigdís decided that she wanted to study the arts in a more serious way. When she finished her basic education at sixteen, she registered at the Reykjavík Grammar School to study language and theater. She also studied in Denmark and France, including at the Sorbonne, an elite school in Paris.

During the summers, she would return to Iceland and work as a tour guide and translator for the Icelandic Tourist Bureau. Her childhood work, answering calls with her mom, meant that she knew a lot about her community, which really helped in this job! When visitors wanted to know about a great place to eat or where to access things along their trips, Vigdís always knew where to point them.

When she was twenty-four years old, Vigdís founded a theater group that translated and performed French plays in Iceland. People in Iceland had never seen these plays before, and they loved them! Vigdís was highly skilled in French and she was hired to give French lessons on the Iceland State Television. What a cool opportunity, Vigdís thought! Just like how she'd been influenced by watching stars like Dorothy in *The Wizard of Oz*, now she, herself, was going to be on TV! Vigdís became well-known—and well-loved—by Icelanders. Total strangers would stop her on the street to say hello. During her years as an actor, Vigdís got married, but the couple divorced a few years later. It was a really hard time for Vigdís, especially because she knew that she wanted to have children. Could she do this on her own, even as a single woman? She decided yes. Vigdís adopted a daughter in 1972, becoming the first single woman in Iceland to officially adopt a child. Life was busy for Vigdís, now running the Reykjavík Theatre Company and taking care of her daughter.

Although the war had been over for years, the Americans and British had set up bases in Iceland. This meant there were still soldiers and military equipment in Iceland, reminding Icelanders about the war. Years went by, and still, they wouldn't go. The Icelandic people wanted their country back and numerous large protests were held. Vigdís was a part of these protests, making her pacifist political views known. This sparked Vigdís's political involvement, and people noticed. It meant something to them, to see such a familiar and beloved face next to them in the crowd. They had learned from Vigdís when she was on TV, and it was inspiring to see her using her voice in a political way. People started asking Vigdís a question: when are you going to run for political office?

Many Icelanders felt that more women needed to be in leadership roles, especially in politics. The country had such a strong history of gender equality, so why has there never been a woman as president or in other key

political roles? Most offices were still held by men—and Icelanders knew that this needed to change. In 1975, tens of thousands of women in Iceland refused to work for one day and, instead, marched outdoors to protest. They wanted more rights for women and better representation of women in leadership roles.

There was a national election coming up. A woman named Laufey from Reykjavík wrote a letter to the editor in the local newspaper saying that a group of women had discussed who should be the next president of Iceland, and they all thought that it should be the director of the local theater—Vigdís. This letter got a lot of people talking! Four days later, the newspaper on a front-page headline said, "Vigdís to stand for president." Vigdís hadn't even agreed to this yet. (And when asked about it earlier, her answer had been no! She was busy with other things and enjoyed the work she was doing.) But this headline got more people talking. Vigdís was getting call after call—almost like when the phone was ringing off the hook at her childhood home, with a community needing her mother's help. When a telegram arrived from the entire crew of a ship out at sea asking her to run, Vigdís knew it was time to answer. And her answer was yes.

The election was held in 1980. When her male opponents questioned whether voters would support a single mother as president, Vigdís was not deterred. Each of these moments just motivated more and more people to get involved in her campaign—and it motivated Vigdís to keep going. She knew that by running, she could help show other girls that anything was possible for them, too. On election night, the results were clear: Vigdís won, with more votes than any of her male opponents. She became the first woman president of Iceland—and the victory was an important global milestone, too. In this victory, Icelanders had supported the first democratically-elected woman president in the entire world.

Vigdís went on to be elected three more times, with strong popularity. In Iceland, it was common that an incumbent president would face no opponents in an election. However, in 1988, an opponent forced Vigdís into an election, which she won with 92.7 per cent of the vote. Vigdís used her time in office to make changes on issues that mattered, including protecting the environment and building a fairer and more equal society in Iceland.

With a presidency of sixteen years, Vigdís is the longest-serving–elected woman head of state in the world. Vigdís's deep belief in gender equality and the capability of women to lead has been expressed in her leadership—reflecting an important part of Icelandic culture. As Vigdís said, "I think if the world can be saved, it will be saved by women."

Prime Minister Saara Kuugongelwa-Amadhila

NAMIBIA

PRIME MINISTER
Saara Kuugongelwa-Amadhila

- Born in Otamanzi, South West Africa (now Namibia), on October 12, 1967
- Spent time in **exile as a child**
- **Studied economics and finance** at university
- Almost **thirty years of service in the National Assembly of Namibia**
- **First woman prime minister of Namibia**, serving from 2015 to 2025

Namibia has a complex history. Its geography is defined by its stunning coastline along the Atlantic Ocean and its deserts. Despite the ocean nearby, Namibia is the driest country in the area. In the 1880s, Namibia was controlled as a colony of the German government. Later, during World War I, the area was claimed by South Africa. It became known as South West Africa. In the 1940s, the South African government imposed its system of apartheid on all its residents. Apartheid is a racist practice where people are discriminated against because of the color of their skin. Even though South West Africa was home to millions of people of many cultural backgrounds speaking over thirty different languages, they were all put into narrow racial categories. In particular, the government limited what Black citizens could do and where they could go. Black kids weren't allowed to go in the "white areas" and had to stay in parts of their communities that didn't have proper schools or hospitals.

Many people knew this was wrong. Citizens in South West Africa wanted to be independent from the government of South Africa and these racist practices. They wanted an end to violence and war, and to be able to chart a more peaceful path forward. International organizations like the United Nations also wanted to see an end to the wars and racism endured by citizens. Finally, in the late 1980s, after years of war and political pressure, South Africa accepted Namibia's independence and agreed to a peace process. Namibia's first democratic elections as an independent nation were held in November 1989. Almost every Namibian (97 per cent) turned out to vote. The winner was the South West Africa People's Organization (SWAPO)—a political party that had been a major voice for the independence movement. They became the government.

As it turned out, some of the leaders of Namibia's independence movement were the very people who had lived through these challenging times—including future prime minister Saara Kuugongelwa-Amadhila.

Saara was born in Otamanzi, a rural community in what was then South West Africa. She was the youngest of five children. Her mother, Alina, was part of the Ondonga—a group of Ovambo people, the dominant ethnic group in Namibia. Her mother was the principal of the local school, and her father worked as a laborer. Life was not easy for Saara and her family. Because of apartheid, there were different rules for Saara than for white children her age. She didn't have access to the same schools or healthcare. She saw how hard this made things for her family. Her father had to travel far away for work doing hard manual labor jobs. She moved to different villages for school and saw terrible things that children should not have to see. Because of the war underway, she saw people who had been taken as prisoners and could hear gunshots as she tried to sleep at night. Both of Saara's parents died in the war when she was a child.

One weekend when Saara was eleven years old, everything changed. Saara's sister, Herta, who was ten years older than Saara, was filled with excitement. She met people from an organization called SWAPO who were pushing for independence. They called the place where they lived "Namibia," not "South West Africa," and imagined a future of independence from South Africa. They were organizing people who supported these ideas, arranging schools and training programs. Herta was all in. She wanted this future, and she wanted to be part of it. When Herta told Saara about these ideas, she

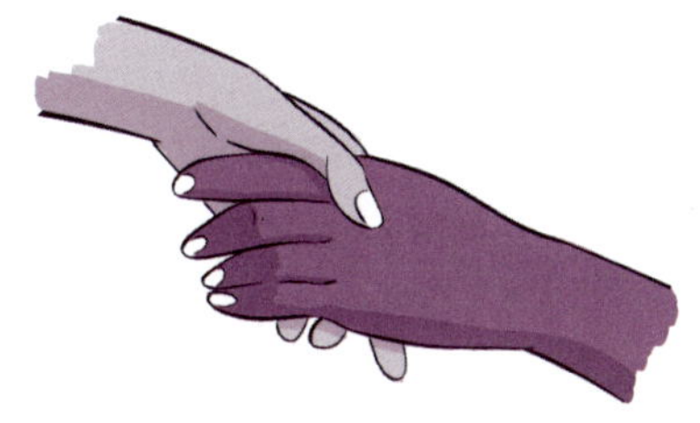

was so excited. It felt good to be hopeful for the future! But could they just leave their home and escape into exile? SWAPO had set up a refugee camp in the neighboring country Angola. It was scary to think about leaving, but the sisters knew that something needed to change. In the middle of the night, Saara and Herta packed their bags and ran for the Angola border.

Life was not easy when they arrived at the SWAPO refugee camp in Angola. The sisters were separated when they arrived, with Herta sent off to military training, and Saara sent to a center for children. It was not exactly what Saara had imagined. Kids at the center got only one meal each day and had to walk over a mile to another camp for lunch. Kids did not have beds or blankets, instead digging trenches in the ground to sleep in at night. Although it was hard, Saara was enjoying learning new things. She learned English and worked hard at her studies. Saara earned a scholarship to attend a girls' school in Sierra Leone. At this school, she met a fourteen-year-old girl whose father was the governor of the central bank in Sierra Leone. What a fascinating job! Saara thought maybe she'd like to do a job like that one day, playing an important role in building the independent country she and Herta had imagined when they escaped together. Saara let this dream motivate her as she continued her studies and completed military training. She finished with the top marks in her school and got a scholarship to go to university in the United States, where she finished with the second-highest marks in her entire university class!

Saara was twenty-one years old when Namibia attained independence. With her academic achievements, international experience, and strong language skills, people in powerful roles noticed Saara and encouraged her to take on leadership roles. She worked directly for the president of Namibia as an economist. She shone in this role—the president himself, Sam Nujoma, noticed her hard work and appointed her to Namibia's parliament as part of the SWAPO political party. By the age of twenty-seven, Saara was the director general of the National Planning Commission, and soon became the minister of finance. Saara loved this role. She got to set up new systems of how Namibia managed its finances, putting the new government—and country—into a stronger financial position. Her staff often joked that she worked the longest hours and carried the heaviest bags of materials home from the office! A few years later, when she was due to give birth, she even answered emails while she was in the hospital having the baby!

In 2015, Saara was elected as the prime minister of Namibia. She is the first woman to lead Namibia's parliament. She served as prime minister for ten years, from 2015 to 2025. Even in this leadership role, Saara never forgot about her childhood struggles. She didn't choose to be born into a violent time under a racist regime where girls had very few opportunities—but she chose how she responded. The choice to escape was brave and difficult, but she was determined to be part of the liberation of her country. She committed her life to building Namibia in hopes that children in the future would not have to experience the things that she did, and where all girls would have the opportunity to pursue their dreams. Many women in Saara's life helped her, including her sister and friends she met in the camps. As a leader, she has tried to pass this on to others. In Saara's words, "Women must support one another. Those of us who have made it must hold the hands of those who are coming, so that they can come not only to where we are but to exceed us."

President Tsai Ing-wen

TAIWAN

PRESIDENT
Tsai Ing-wen

- Born in Taipei City, Taiwan, on August 31, 1956
- **Studied law and economics**, earning a PhD in law
- **First woman president of Taiwan**, serving from 2016 to 2024
- Known for being an **animal lover**, with two cats who have appeared in her campaign videos, and three retired guide dogs

Tsai Ing-wen knows what it's like to be underestimated. She was born in 1956 in a hospital in Taipei City, the capital of Taiwan. In fact, she was born in a place that has often been underestimated. How did a shy little girl who never imagined herself in politics grow up to become the first (and only) president of Taiwan, playing an important role in changing Taiwan's place in the world?

Ing-wen's story begins in Taipei City, the bustling capital of the pacific island of Taiwan. The streets were filled with people, bicycles, and the sounds of a busy city! Sometimes it was a bit overwhelming for Ing-wen. As a little girl, she would sometimes drop her head to look at the ground when people walked by. She liked being quiet and playing on her own. Sometimes, grown-ups would ask her what she wanted to be when she grew up. This was a tough question for Ing-wen. She liked history and nature and learning about the world. Sometimes, she would play outside and pretend to be doing an archaeological dig, quietly digging in the ground while other kids played and ran around her. She would think to herself, it would be fun to learn about archaeology and history—and because people in history lived a long time ago, there would be no one she would have to talk to!

It was hard to be a shy kid in a busy city with a big family. There were always people around. Ing-wen was the youngest kid in her family, with ten older brothers and sisters. Her father, Tsai Chieh-sheng, was a businessman who knew a lot of people in their city. He grew up in a rural area of Taiwan and was sent away to study mechanical maintenance with the help of family and friends when he was eighteen—mostly to avoid being forced into the military by the Japanese in World War II. After the war, Chieh-sheng decided to settle in Taipei City where he opened a car repair business. This turned out to be a good business move, and his car business made enough money to start investing in real estate. Ing-wen's mother, Chang Chin-fong, stayed home to take care of the children. The couple believed strongly in education for all their children, and Chieh-sheng shared his wealth by creating a library and donating hundreds of thousands of books in his home community.

Sometimes, it felt like a lot of pressure to be the youngest kid in a big family. Ing-wen's father encouraged all of his kids to learn about the law and the world around them. He'd seen just how much politics can matter, given the big changes that happened in Taiwan during his lifetime. Over Taiwan's history, it has been colonized by many other countries including periods of Dutch, Spanish, Japanese, and Chinese rule. During Chieh-sheng's life, Taiwan struggled to achieve independence and chart its own path forward. The rule of other countries meant that Taiwan was exploited or had to adapt to rigid customs from other places. As a business owner, Chieh-sheng knew how important these changes could be to people's lives and how successful people could actually be in their business ventures, so he wanted his children to learn about politics and the law. And as Ing-wen's siblings chose other paths, her father talked to her about pursuing a degree in law.

Ing-wen was a smart kid. She did well at school and loved learning new things. Her childhood dream of being an archaeologist sounded like a path to the quiet life she wanted for herself, but her father's encouragement changed her mind. Ing-wen completed her high school years at the all-girls' school in Taipei City and decided to do a degree in law at the National Taiwan University.

Ing-wen excelled in her studies, but sometimes, the Taiwan school system felt too rigid. Her classes were filled with boys, and she questioned some of the things she was learning. In her studies, she learned about other country's political and economic systems and started to imagine how things could be different for people in Taiwan under different sets of rules. After spending her whole life in Taiwan, she decided it was time to broaden her experience and perspective. She had very good marks and was accepted into Cornell Law School in the United States and moved around the world to complete another degree in law—much to the delight of her father, getting her second degree in this field!

Life in the United States was very different, as a democratic country built on the idea of freedom—where people can choose their own destiny—and has broken away from colonial rule to be an independent nation. Learning about the law in a new place and within a new context was eye opening. At the end of her degree, Ing-wen decided to make another big move: she moved to the United Kingdom to complete a PhD at the prestigious London School of Economics. She then returned home to Taipei City and taught at a law school.

Even though she was still a shy person, being a professor was a great fit for Ing-wen. As a professor, she had to learn to speak in front of other people—this was now something that she did every day! Her students learned so much from her. Ing-wen's calm and clear way of explaining complex things helped her students understand the law. She wasn't the loudest or most dynamic speaker, but she learned how to speak in a way that connected with her students. She noticed that when she would walk up to the podium in her classroom, the students would all quiet down because they didn't want to miss a word that she said. She became known as a smart professor and a clear and articulate communicator.

These skills and abilities made people notice Ing-wen. She was a legal expert and understood international relations, in part because she'd lived and studied the law in different parts of the world. One day, Ing-wen was approached

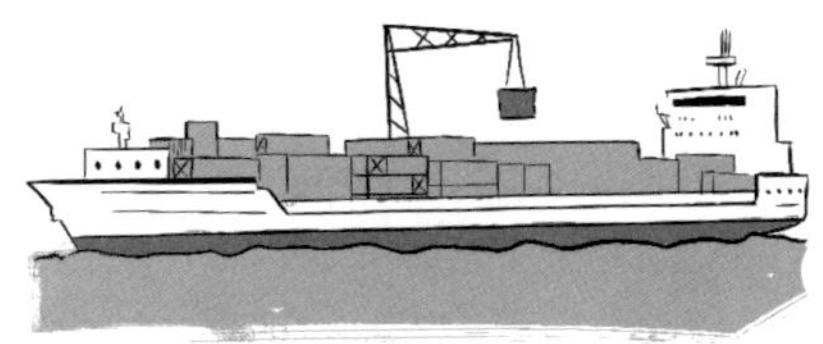

about a big opportunity: she was appointed to the Fair Trade Commission, an organization giving advice to the government about how to negotiate new relationships with other countries to benefit businesses and growth in Taiwan. Ing-wen thought about her father and his successes. He wanted her to study law so she could make things better for people in Taiwan, including entrepreneurs who started their own businesses. This was a chance for her to do exactly this.

This drive and passion helped Ing-wen be very successful in this role—so successful that an even bigger opportunity came her way. She was only thirty-seven when she was invited to serve on the International Trade Commission for Taiwan, leading international negotiations and the National Security Council to give advice to the president of Taiwan on security and relations with China. All of a sudden, Ing-wen's life changed a lot. Her days used to be spent in law classrooms speaking to her students, and now she was flying off to important meetings in Washington (the capital of the United States) and other political centers to talk about Taiwan's political status. Other politicians would comment on Ing-wen's skill and praised her for her ability to represent Taiwan on an international stage. Her calm, thoughtful, and well-informed way of handling even the most difficult of discussions turned out to be very effective.

Ing-wen never imagined herself in politics, but these roles taught her just how important the decisions made by political leaders were in shaping people's quality of life. She loved Taiwan. She wanted to see a more modern, more progressive, and more democratic Taiwan in the future. If she could do more to make this vision a reality, would she? For Ing-wen, the answer to this question was clear: yes.

In 2004, Ing-wen decided to join a political party, the Democratic Progressive Party (DPP), and run in an election. She won, and Ing-wen rose to an important leadership role as the vice president of the Executive Yuan (also

called vice premier) in 2006. In 2008, she decided to go for the top role. She ran and won a leadership race and led her party in an election. On election night, Ing-wen was surrounded by cheering supporters. Just as she had when she was a professor, she walked calmly to the podium. People quieted to hear what she had to say. Ing-wen didn't need to try to be like every other president; being true to herself and her style is what made her so successful.

The people of Taiwan hadn't elected a woman president before, and a few things about her were also different. Ing-wen was not married and did not have children—something that was also a first for a Taiwanese president. Ing-wen loved her two cats, Think Think and Ah Tsai, who become popular after being featured in her political videos and social media posts!

Ing-wen has made many important changes in Taiwan. She is especially known for being a supporter of LGBTQ rights. In 2019, she signed a bill that made same-sex marriage legal—making Taiwan the first country in Asia to do so. Ing-wen was also the first Taiwanese president to march in pride parades, and she appointed Taiwan's first transgender and non-binary cabinet minister. During the COVID pandemic, Ing-wen's calm and methodical approach once again turned out to be very useful as she led the country through crisis with a clear plan and a steady leadership style.

In Ing-wen's words, "The greatness of Taiwan lies in how every single person can exercise their right to be themselves." Being a shy kid doesn't mean that paths like politics are impossible; being in a place that has faced many challenges doesn't mean that a better future isn't possible. Sometimes, being underestimated can turn out to be a powerful place to start.

Chancellor Angela Merkel

GERMANY

CHANCELLOR Angela Merkel

- Born in Hamburg, West Germany (now Germany), on July 17, 1954
- Worked as a **scientist before entering politics**; holds a PhD in quantum chemistry
- Served as the **chancellor of Germany** from 2005 to 2021, and is the only woman to hold this position
- Widely considered one of the **most influential leaders in Europe** and one of the most powerful women in the world

Imagine a big wall running right through the middle of a city, almost fifteen feet high and more than ninety-three miles long! Kids who lived in West Germany and East Germany in the 1960s didn't have to imagine this; they lived it. They saw the Berlin Wall go up and divide their city in two, separating families and neighbors and making it harder for people to move around freely in and around the city of Berlin. After World War II, Germany was a divided country. Nations that won the war took control of different regions. East Berlin was in East Germany, with a harsh and controlling government. West Berlin was in West Germany. While many families desperately tried to get across the border into West Germany, one couple and their three-month-old baby were headed in the opposite direction: into East Germany. This little girl would grow up to become the chancellor of Germany, now known as one of the most powerful women in the world. Who was this girl?

Angela Dorothea Kasner was born in 1954 in Hamburg, one of Germany's major cities. Much of the city had been destroyed or damaged by bombs during World War II, but by the time Angela was born, citizens had begun the long task of rebuilding. Angela's mother, Herlind, was an English and Latin teacher. Angela's father, Horst Kasner, was a theologian, which is a person who studies religion. Her parents had met while Horst was studying theology in Hamburg. Herlind and Horst married, and shortly after, Herlind gave birth to their first child, Angela.

When Angela was just three months old, her father got a new job at a church in East Germany, not too far from the country's capital of Berlin. This meant that they would have to leave the safety of West Germany, but they were dedicated to their religious beliefs and felt it was necessary to support others in the same faith. So, they went past fences and border guards and entered East Germany.

The young family lived in a place called the Waldhof, where there was a complex of homes and farm buildings. It was founded in 1852 as a home for young people with disabilities. The Waldhof also played an important role for the church, as it was used to house people who needed support and run the business of the church.

Angela's dad was asked to set up a new college at the Waldhof for church administrators. He also taught there. At one point, every pastor in the church had passed through the college, having been taught by Horst Kasner. Horst, Herlind, and Angela lived at the Waldhof for many years, welcoming two younger siblings while they lived there.

For most of Germany, the years following World War II were busy. It was a difficult time in Germany in the wake of war; a period of turmoil and change and rebuilding. But for Angela, life inside the Waldhof was quite calm. It was almost like they were secluded on a deserted island, far from the concerns of regular society. Angela did not attend kindergarten but, instead, played alongside people at the Waldhof who worked as gardeners or cooks. She would run around their legs, chasing one of the other kids and sometimes helped them plant in the garden with a little shovel and watering can. Angela later described it as a "place that gave children space."

Her family dining table was often packed with people. Her father's students and other people from the church would join in their family meals. They would have intense political conversations that went on late into the night. Angela was seven years old when the Berlin Wall was built, a physical barrier dividing the city of Berlin in two: East and West. The Wall became a central topic of conversation among the grown-ups, especially since Berlin was so close by. Angela's parents had sensed that something was changing, particularly when they saw rolls of barbed wire stacked in a forest along the highway that connected East and West Berlin. Angela's parents cried as they saw those rolls of barbed wire turn into a huge wall that separated them from their friends and families. Angela's mom sobbed all day, worried that she might never see her family in Hamburg again. Guards and soldiers controlled the checkpoints along the wall as people tried to escape East Germany.

Life in East Germany was harsh, but Angela was thankful for the solace of the Waldhof. There, she had access to something highly restricted for other kids: books! Angela's parents had a vast library, which became her escape during these dark times. She learned to read in different languages and found stories that captured her imagination. It was here she met a new hero: scientist Marie Curie, the first woman to win a Nobel Prize (and later a second one!). Just like Angela, Marie was of Polish descent and lived in a country that was divided and occupied by a controlling government. Marie rose above this to focus on science. Marie famously said, "Nothing in life is to be feared, it is only to be understood." Angela found this inspiring and felt science could be a powerful way for her to make sense of the world around her, too.

As Angela got older, she became more defiant toward life in East Germany. The government was too controlling, not just limiting where people could go and what they could read, but also what they wore. As a young teenager, Angela's family in Hamburg had found a way to get a special treat to her: blue jeans! She wore her new jeans to school and got in trouble for sporting something that was viewed to be a symbol of the Western world. She also secretly followed politics in West Germany, once sneaking into a school bathroom with a small radio to listen to West German election results. Angela was known as a very smart student, and she did well in school. She won a language Olympics competition when

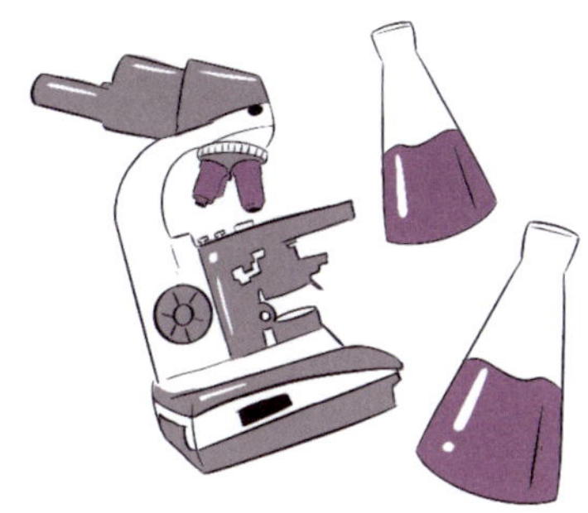

she was fifteen years old, earning her a scholarship to attend a more prestigious high school and a path to exit East Germany.

At university, Angela was an excellent student. She studied physics and chemistry, earning a PhD. While she was a student, she met and fell in love with a physics student. They married in 1977 when Angela was twenty-three. The couple divorced a few years later, but Angela kept his last name: Merkel. Angela later married a quantum chemist and professor with two children. Angela worked as a researcher for the Central Institute for Physical Chemistry at the Academy of Sciences, publishing several important research papers as she became a more well-known scientist.

In November 1989, the Berlin Wall fell. Citizens on each side of the Wall tore parts of the wall down themselves and climbed over it to reunite with loved ones who had been on the opposite side. The Wall's destruction marked the fall of communism in central and eastern Europe, and the reunification of Germany. For Angela, this was a major moment in her life. Suddenly, it felt like there were new opportunities and possibilities that didn't exist before. She decided she wanted to be a part of building the future of the newly united Germany.

Within a month of the Berlin Wall coming down, Angela joined a political party. People could see that Angela was smart and good at communicating, including in several languages. She became the person who would speak to the media, taking on new leadership roles within the party. A year later, Germany was going to have its first federal election since the country had reunited. Angela decided that she wanted to do everything she could to help the future of Germany. She ran for office in the election and was elected to parliament. Shortly after, she was named minister for women and youth. She served in other leadership roles, too, including as minister of the environment, chairperson and general secretary of her party, and eventually, leader of the opposition. In these roles, she got to make important decisions about how Germany would address climate change or help kids receive a better education. It was busy but rewarding, with Angela often thinking back to the divisions that shaped her own childhood as a motivation for how to make things better.

In 2005, Angela led her party in the general election. After building a grand coalition of three political parties to govern, she was elected chancellor—the most senior and important political role for all of Germany, and an important role within Europe. Angela was the first woman to hold the role and served as chancellor for sixteen years, from 2005 to 2021, leading her country through some challenging times. During the COVID pandemic, her background as a scientist was particularly helpful in making evidence-based political decisions to protect the health and lives of German citizens.

Like her childhood hero Marie Curie, Angela's intelligence and relentless curiosity about the world around her led her to amazing achievements. While serving as chancellor, Angela once said, "The question is not whether we are able to change but whether we are changing fast enough." Like Marie, seeing what *can be* and beyond *what is* has been an important part of Angela's contribution to her country and to the world.

Prime Minister and Acting President Sylvie Kinigi

BURUNDI

PRIME MINISTER AND ACTING PRESIDENT
Sylvie Kinigi

- Born in Mugoyi, Ruanda-Urundi (now Burundi), on November 24, 1953
- Worked in **banking** before entering politics
- Served as the **prime minister and acting president of Burundi** from 1993 to 1994
- **Second African woman to serve as president**

Burundi is an African country with a humid tropical climate. Part of the country sits along the beautiful Lake Tanganyika, one of the African Great Lakes—and the largest source of fresh water in Africa. Burundi is a very young country (the average age of citizens is just over sixteen years old), with a current population of just over fourteen million people.

Burundi's history has been shaped by struggles for power. The two dominant ethnic groups, the Hutu and the Tutsi people, have lived in what is now Burundi for more than five hundred years. This includes periods as an independent kingdom and periods under German and Belgian colonial rule. The Hutu and Tutsi people were considered to have different social statuses, with the Tutsi having higher status and greater wealth. The foreign colonizers took this social division and made laws around them. The Hutu and Tutsis were forced to follow different rules. This created even more tension between them. Conflicts between foreign colonial powers, as well as between ethnic groups, became common. Many generations of people were forced to live through one war after another, and they even faced genocide. Both Burundi and neighboring Rwanda achieved independence in the early 1960s. People were hopeful that this would mean an end to war and violence. Unfortunately, it was not. The newly independent nation became a monarchy led by a family dynasty. This meant that instead of getting to vote for their leader, the people of Burundi would have to follow the rule of one powerful family. It felt like a step backward, and many were unhappy. More conflicts followed. Competing ethnic groups tried to seize power. For decades, the people of Burundi have endured unimaginable violence and loss of life.

One person who has lived this experience is Sylvie Kinigi, the first woman to serve as both prime minister and president of Burundi—and the second African woman to serve as a president. How did a girl born into such a difficult time and place rise above all to lead her country?

Sylvie was born in Mugoyi, a rural community in the western countryside of what was then called Ruanda-Urundi. She was the third of six children in her family. Sylvie's family was part of the Tutsi peoples, a significant ethnic group in the African Great Lakes region. Her father worked as a merchant, and her mother farmed and stayed home to look after the children. Sylvie's oldest sister was not allowed to attend school. Instead, she had to stay home to help her mother look after the house and the younger children. A new school was just being built, and the timing ended up being lucky for Sylvie, as she got to do something that her older sister didn't: she got to go to school.

Sylvie was nine years old when Burundi achieved independence from Belgium. As people began to create a new government system, there were many problems. Even though there were more Hutu than Tutsi people in Burundi, the Tutsi remained powerful just as they had been before independence. More fights broke out between the two groups, and it seemed that there would be no end to the conflict. The Burundi government was controlled by Tutsi military officers for decades.

When Sylvie was twenty years old, she married Firmin Kinigi, an academic who later became head librarian at the University of Burundi. But the thing was, Firmin was Hutu, and Sylvie was Tutsi. While marriages between Hutus and Tutsis had been common before colonization, things were very different now. Sylvie knew that one marriage wouldn't change the world, but it did show people that it was possible for the two groups to unite despite their differences. Together, the couple

had five children. Firmin believed that Sylvie should continue her education even after having children and encouraged her to do so. At the time, this broke gender norms, which insisted that women stay home and raise the children on their own. Firmin and Sylvie decided to hire help to care for the home and their children so Sylvie could continue her studies.

Sylvie attended the University of Burundi to study economics and banking. She also moved to Paris for a year to complete a diploma in banking. On returning home to Burundi, she was hired to work at a central banking agency. She also taught courses at the University of Burundi. Her talents and capable leadership over complex files led her to a quick rise: first, into the office of the prime minister to lead negotiations with the International Monetary Fund and World Bank; then, as a leader in the ministry of economic planning.

It was a significant time to be in government in Burundi as the nation tried to make a shift toward peace and democracy. In 1988, the Burundi government released a report on the loss of life and implications of the longstanding Hutu–Tutsi conflict and convened a Commission of National Unity. Their report and recommendations were presented in 1989, leading to the creation of a new central agency to lead the country to democracy and bridge ethnic divides. A new charter and later constitution were presented to citizens to vote on through referendums (in 1991 and then 1992), yielding a high voter turnout (above 90 per cent) and high levels of support (around 90 per cent) for the proposed constitutional changes. The 1992 referendum introduced a new model for governing: a presidential model with five-year terms; the introduction of proportional representation for electing the parliament, guarantees for freedom of the press, and a requirement for political parties to accept the Charter of National Unity.

This made possible an important step forward in June 1993: Burundi's first multi-party democratic elections (previous "elections" had only one political party option). This marked an end to the Tutsi military domination in Burundi, with a Hutu leader, Melchior Ndadaye, elected as president. Melchior won with 66 per cent of the votes, and a 97 per cent voter turnout.

Shortly after the election, Melchior made an important choice: he appointed Sylvie, a Tutsi, to serve as his prime minister. Not everyone was happy with this. Some felt that Melchior was betraying the Hutu-based party and their supporters. Others recognized that it was a political strategy. An intelligent Tutsi woman in a position of power would be appealing for both Tutsi citizens and women in general. Sylvie became the first woman prime minister of Burundi. She announced that her top priority in the role would be to focus on reconciling the Hutus and the Tutsis. She began a process to engage political leaders in listening, learning, and healing from the significant conflicts and traumas of the past.

Unfortunately, Sylvie was ahead of her time. Not everyone was ready to move forward, so this work was short-lived. Just three months after the election, Melchior and several other officials were killed by Tutsi soldiers in an effort to take over the government. Sylvie's bodyguards remained loyal to her and helped her survive the attack. Because she was the highest-ranking political official still alive, Sylvie became the president of Burundi. She took refuge at the French embassy for some time and then returned to Burundi with police officers to protect her. She focused on stabilizing the conflict, but once again, the level of violence was out of control. She asked international bodies to help her stabilize the situation. Then, she focused her energy on getting a new president elected as quickly as possible. Once the new president was in place, she resigned from office.

Sylvie's experiences taught her many important lessons, including how important education is to unlocking possibilities in people's lives. This is especially important for girls in areas where access to education is still limited. If a new school hadn't been built at exactly the right time and place when Sylvie was a child, and if her parents hadn't supported sending her to school at a time when it was not common, would she have become president? Education unlocks futures. Even after her time in politics, Sylvie has continued to work toward rights for women and girls through roles with the United Nations. In Sylvie's words, "The fight for human rights must always push forward."

Vice President Kamala Harris

UNITED STATES OF AMERICA

VICE PRESIDENT
Kamala Harris

- Born in Oakland, USA, on October 20, 1964
- Raised by a single mom and moved with her little sister to many different places as a child, including places in the USA and in Canada
- Studied **political science**, **economics**, and **law**
- **First woman, first African American, and first Asian American** to serve as **vice president of the United States of America**
- **Ran for president of the United States** of America in 2024

The United States of America (USA) is one of the largest nations in the world, in both population and land. For decades, people have come from all over the world to pursue the "American Dream": freedom, opportunity, and a better life for their family. The country gained its independence from Britain almost 250 years ago, and since then, it has become an economic and military powerhouse. Now, American culture influences people around the world. To date, Americans have never elected a woman president. However, two women have come very close: Hillary Clinton in 2016, and Kamala Harris in 2024. Kamala was the first woman to serve as vice president of the United States. Out of a population of 350 million, what enabled one girl to become the first woman American vice president? Like so many Americans, Kamala's story begins abroad.

Kamala's mother, Shyamala Gopalan, was born in 1938 in Madras, British India, which is now called Chennai, India. Her family was Tamil Hindu. Shyamala was the oldest of four children. She was a gifted singer and had a passion for science. It wasn't common for girls to go to university at the time and almost unheard of for them to go abroad. But Shyamala's parents encouraged her to attend school, and when she announced that she wanted to attend the University of California, Berkeley, in the United States of America, her parents supported her. It was a very brave move for a teenager who had never traveled outside of India. At Berkeley, Shyamala studied with a goal to become a breast cancer researcher. Her parents at home did not have a landline phone, so Shyamala communicated with them by writing letters.

As a student, Shyamala got involved in the Civil Rights Movement, which fought for equal rights for Black people. In 1962, she attended a meeting of the Afro-American student association at Berkeley. There, she met Donald Harris, who was giving a presentation that day. Donald had been born in Brown's Town, Jamaica, and had come to the United States to do a PhD. Shyamala and Donald had a lot in common. They both had a passion for music and loved learning. A year later, Shyamala and Donald got married. In 1964, Shyamala graduated with a PhD, and she and Donald had their first child: Kamala Devi Harris. What a year!

Kamala and her parents lived in Berkeley, California. It was a happy time. Their little family of three quickly became a family of four with the birth of Kamala's younger sister, Maya, in 1967. The next year, Donald accepted a teaching job at the University of Wisconsin. That meant he had to move away from his family. Because of this move, Shyamala and Donald grew apart. They separated and then divorced shortly after—leaving Shyamala to raise two young girls, Kamala and Maya, largely on her own. They lived in the top floor of a duplex in a working-class neighborhood.

Shyamala believed in political activism: standing up for the things she believed in to make life better for others. She made sure her girls understood why it was so important. She told them stories about their grandmother in India, and how she didn't have the opportunity to attend high school but still found ways to help her community. She would help neighbors in any way she could, sometimes helping women who were being abused by their husbands to leave and find safety. Kamala thought these stories were so inspiring. Imagine be-

ing able to help people in their times of need! To Kamala, this sounded like the most important thing a person could do. Kamala had other inspirations, too. Shyamala also brought Kamala and her sister to civil rights rallies. They even got to hear Martin Luther King Jr. speak at Berkeley. Shyamala made close friends with other women who attended these rallies. They became aunties and godmothers to Kamala and Maya, helping raise them. Between school, church, and time at the Black cultural center, Rainbow Sign, Kamala learned about the civil rights movement. Shyamala would often tell her girls, "Fight systems in a way that causes them to be fairer, and don't be limited by what has always been."

In the 1960s, there was a national program to eliminate segregation in education (a harmful law that prevented Black students from going to the same schools as white students). For Kamala, this meant that she and Maya would get on a big, yellow school bus in the morning with other Black children from working class families and ride to a neighborhood with wealthier, white children. Kamala didn't understand yet what a significant change this was; for her, it simply meant that she had friends from different backgrounds who lived in different neighborhoods.

When Kamala was twelve years old, her mother accepted a job at McGill University in Montréal, Canada. Kamala was not happy about moving from sunny California to a much colder city that spoke a different language, in a different country! At their new school in Montréal, Kamala and Maya were discouraged to find that there were also new rules—including that kids were not allowed to play soccer on the school's lawn. Kamala and Maya thought this was ridiculous! They talked to their classmates and quickly learned that other kids didn't like this rule either. Kamala, Maya, and their classmates decided to hold a protest in front of the school property

to challenge this rule—and it worked! The school leaders paid attention, and shortly after, the rule was changed.

That was just the start of things for Kamala. At Westmount High School in Montreal, Kamala met a new friend, Wanda. They joined a dance troupe called Midnight Magic together. But Kamala began to notice some concerning things about her friend. Wanda shared that she was being abused at home. Kamala went to her mother and asked if Wanda could move in with them. Shyamala said yes, and together, their family helped Wanda escape danger. For Kamala, this was an important lesson: just like her grandmother and mother, she wanted to spend her life helping people—and particularly those who were facing injustices. By speaking up and standing up for what is right, she could help the people who needed it most. This experience was transformative for Kamala. It gave her a strong desire to protect people—particularly women and children.

Kamala knew what she wanted to do. By studying law and working in the justice system, she could help and protect people like her friend, Wanda. She went to Howard University, a historically Black university in Washington, DC, to study politics and economics. She then went to law school at the University of California, and then started working as a lawyer for the government. One Friday afternoon, Kamala was reviewing files and noticed that one of the cases at the bottom of the pile was about a young mother. She knew that the judge wouldn't be able to get to that case before the day was done, which meant that the mother would have to wait until the next week for a decision. Kamala thought about what this would mean for this mother: a weekend away from her kids, and a challenge for the whole family. What if she could ask the judge to look at this case before the weekend? Kamala decided to go for it. She brought the case forward for review, and in doing so, this mother was able to spend the weekend with her children. It felt so good for Kamala to know that her work was helping people and their families.

Kamala rose to more senior and important roles. Sometimes, she was the first Black woman to be in those roles. She was often underestimated, but Kamala was never deterred. She remembered the examples of her grandmother and her mother and stayed focused. She remembered her mother telling her, "You may be the first to do many things but make sure you're not the last." Kamala persisted. She became a prosecutor so she could advocate for victims. As a prosecutor, she put people who broke the law in jail. Then, she realized if she wanted to make better laws to protect more people, she needed to get involved in politics.

In 2016, Kamala was elected to the US Senate as the second Black woman and first South Asian American to serve in the Senate. She then ran to be the Democratic Party's candidate for president in 2020. Although she was not successful, she was selected by the winner, Joe Biden, to be his running mate. In 2020, Joe Biden and Kamala Harris defeated the incumbent president and won the election, making Kamala the first woman to serve as vice president of the United States. It was not an easy time, including facing a global pandemic—but Kamala stayed focused on what brought her into politics in the first place. She was there to help people.

In 2024, it was time once again for Americans to have an election. In the summer of 2024, President Biden decided that he was not going to seek reelection. What did that mean for Kamala's party? Who would be the party's candidate for president? President Biden had a clear answer; he thought the next president should be Kamala. Lots of people agreed! Within twenty-four hours, key leaders in the party all across the country chimed in with their support to see Kamala run for president. She raised more money than any other candidate in her party's history. She spoke to crowds across America, talking about the things she wanted to do as president, like protecting women's rights and making America a more equal place. Every time Kamala would speak, little girls in the audience would have tears in their eyes as they chanted, "Kamala! Kamala! Kamala!" Just like her mother told her, you may be the first, but make sure you're not the last.

Although more than seventy-five million people voted for Kamala, it wasn't quite enough. Kamala was not elected as president. The day after the election, Kamala spoke to a huge crowd of supporters—many in tears, disappointed about her loss. It would have been easy to feel angry or sad, but Kamala walked on stage with her head held high and reminded her supporters to keep pushing for the change they wanted to see: "This is not a time to throw up our hands, it's a time to roll up our sleeves." Until Americans elect a woman as president; until all Americans enjoy equal rights and opportunities; until all girls can achieve their biggest dreams, the fight for justice must continue.

Onward.

Conclusion

Billions of kids have lived on our planet. They have accomplished many amazing things. A very small group of these kids grew up to become political leaders and make decisions that shaped the lives of the people around them. Almost all of these kids were boys.

This book has featured a few stories of girls who defied this pattern, growing up to become the president or prime minister of their country. They broke glass ceilings, shattered expectations, and set new norms. In doing so, they showed us that girls and women *can*, *should*, and *must* lead.

There are a lot of differences between the girls featured in these pages. They have lived at different times and in different places. Their families were different—some were the only children in their families, while others were part of big families. Some of these girls were born into important political families. They had to break the mold by becoming the first woman in a lineage of male leaders to hold top political roles. Others grew up in working-class families, had single mothers, lived on farms, and even escaped into exile. Many faced injustices and tragedies along their journeys.

These girls shared a few very important things in common.

First, they loved their country. They believed in their country. To them, being a citizen of their country was an active decision to be engaged. They spoke up. They got involved. Some of them protested for peace, democracy, and freedom. Others found ways to turn tragic experiences into a motivation to help others.

Questions for you:

- Do you think the girls described in this book have anything in common? What was different about their stories?
- What kinds of privileges did some of the girls in this book enjoy? What oppressions did they experience? How did this shape their political careers?
- Have you ever experienced an injustice—a rule or decision or action that was unfair to a group of people, or that helped some people but hurt others? What did you want to do to help?
- Why is politics important? Why does it matter who holds political leadership roles?

Second, these girls knew that they could lead change. Sometimes, the people around them didn't believe this, or needed some time to be convinced that a woman could lead in a role that had only ever been held by men. The leaders in this book were not discouraged. They persisted.

Third, for these women, it was not about the job; it was about the changes they wanted to see happen in their countries and in the world. They got the top jobs because they were willing to step forward and try to make change, even when it was hard or when the odds were stacked against them. They accomplished many amazing things that have helped people around the world.

In a democracy, every person has a role to play. We have power over the things that matter to us. The people who step forward to lead have a huge opportunity to make things better for those around them. All of the girls in this book stepped forward to lead. They didn't wait until they were in the top jobs to start pushing for changes; they pushed when they believed that changes were needed. They started when they were kids.

Our world needs more of that. We need more girls to lead.

You don't need to change who you are, or what you look like, or where you're from, or what skills and talents and interests you have in order to become a leader. All you need is to find what you are passionate about and what changes you want to see in your country—and then *we* need *you* to act.

You can show up.

You can step up.

You can speak up.

You can run the world like a girl.

Glossary of Terms

Apartheid: A political system that separates people (often called segregation) based on race, where some people have fewer rights, are treated worse, or have fewer opportunities than other people, simply because of who they are.

Cabinet: A group of people, often members from the governing *political party*, who make decisions about what a government is going to do on specific things like healthcare, education, justice, or the economy. The members of the cabinet are often called cabinet ministers.

Candidate: A person who runs for political office (sometimes referred to as a "political candidate"), including in a democratic *election* where citizens can vote for the candidate they want to represent them in government.

Civil Rights Movement: A campaign in the United States to gain rights for African American people and to abolish unfair systems of *discrimination* where Black Americans experienced oppression and did not have access to the same supports or opportunities as white people.

Coalition: A temporary decision for different political parties to work together to accomplish things they share an interest in leading (for example, healthcare improvements). The point of a coalition is that, by coming together, the new group can hold the most seats in a legislature or parliament, allowing them to form a government and make decisions.

Colonial: A system where one country or empire has control over another territory.

Communism: Can mean a form of government or a political theory (an idea about how governments and societies should work), where the government owns things like land, buildings, businesses, and wealth.

Constitution: The set of laws, rules, and conventions that set out the powers of government in a country.

Democracy: A system of government where power is shared by all people, and where people vote for their elected representatives to make decisions on their behalf.

Diplomat: An official who represents their country in other nations.

Discrimination: An unfair, unjust, or prejudiced treatment of different categories of people on the basis of gender, ethnicity, culture, race, disability, sexual orientation, age, and more.

Dynasty: When several people in the same family are important leaders in a government or political party, usually over a long period of time. A monarchy can be an example of this, where kids grow up to become rulers or leaders because their parents were also rulers.

Egalitarian: A belief that all people are equal and should not face *discrimination* because of who they are.

Election: An opportunity for citizens to vote for the person they want to represent them in government.

Exile: To be barred from your own country.

Gender roles: Social and cultural expectations for how people will behave based on their assigned sex.

Glass ceiling: A phrase used to describe an invisible barrier that prevents a group of people, such as women, from reaching the highest roles in an organization or government.

Govern: Refers to making decisions and controlling, directing, or influencing outcomes.

Government: The group of people who make decisions and rules about a country or community. Some of the people are elected (like *prime ministers* or *members of parliament*) and some are not elected (like deputy ministers, directors-general, or program officers). The elected officials make decisions on how to raise funds from the public (usually through taxes) and how to spend those funds (on things like healthcare, national or provincial parks, and social supports) and pass laws.

Human rights: The rights that all human beings have and that cannot be given or taken away by any government. Human rights include things like freedom from slavery and torture, freedom of opinion, the right to education, and many more.

Incumbent: A person who is already in a certain role or job, such as being the prime minister.

Intersectionality: The way that various parts of each person's identity, including race, class, gender, and more, overlap within patterns or systems of privilege and oppression.

Leadership race: An election within a political party to determine who will be the leader of the party. Usually, only members or supporters of the party may vote in the leadership race.

Majority government: A government run by a political party that has a majority of the seats.

Marxism: An idea about how society should work, based on the work of a German philosopher named Karl Marx, where wealth is shared between workers and those who own businesses.

Mayor: The head of a local council, usually elected directly by voters in the municipality or community.

Member of parliament (MP): A person elected by the eligible voters in a specific area to represent them in the government. An MP also helps the people in their area navigate government programs.

Military coup: An illegal attempt to overthrow the government by the country's military organization.

Pacifist: A person who opposes war and violence.

Parliament: A specific part of a government usually referring to the people who were elected to pass laws.

Political party: An organization, usually made up of members or supporters, who share common values and ideas for how to run a province, state, or country. Political parties nominate or put forward candidates in federal and provincial elections.

Politics: The way that a country or group is governed, particularly how rules and decisions are made. Politics is about how power is used: who holds power, over what, and how it is used.

President: The leader of a country and top political official. In a republic, the president is often elected by citizens. In a parliamentary system, citizens may elect a legislature and who then appoint a president. Some countries have a president and a prime minister; other countries have one or the other.

Prime minister: In a parliamentary system, the top political official and person elected by citizens to lead the government. Most countries with a prime minister also have a head of state, such as the Queen or King (in places like Canada) or the president (in places like Pakistan).

Privilege: Something that benefits some people and not others, such as wealth or being part of a dominant group.

Proportional representation: An election system where political parties hold a certain number of seats based on the percentage of the votes they receive. This is different from a first-past-the-post majority model, where the party winning the highest number of seats holds the most power (even if they received a much lower percentage of overall votes).

Public service: A broad term that refers to non-elected government employees.

Referendum: A general vote by citizens in a country on a single political question.

Socialism: A form of government and political theory emphasizing common ownership of wealth.

Stereotype: A widely held idea about something or someone that is usually based on appearances and is often untrue. Stereotypes can be harmful and are sometimes used to discriminate against certain groups of people.

Underrepresentation: Can refer to the limited access or participation of a group of people. In politics, this term often refers to groups of people who are not included in specific roles such as elected officials.

United Nations: An international organization of countries founded in 1945 that works to promote peace, security, and human rights in countries around the world.

Vote: In an election, the act of picking which candidate should be chosen as the representative for a specific area or community.

Acknowledgments

This book emerged out of a project called *No Second Chances*, which examines the rise and fall of women political leaders in Canada. *No Second Chances* was produced by the wonderful team at Canada 2020, generously supported by Mastercard Canada and Margaret McCain. Second Story Press published two books on this project: *No Second Chances*, an adult book comprised of interviews with Canada's first women ministers; and, *Govern Like a Girl*, a children's book about the girls who would grow up to lead in Canada.

This book, *Run the World Like a Girl*, builds on this work by exploring the origin stories of women leaders from around the world. In some cases—Kim Campbell, Michelle Bachelet, Sylvie Kinigi, and Saara Kuugongelwa-Amadhila—this book was informed by interviews with the leaders featured. In all cases, the book was informed by research on each leader with interest in drawing on what we know of their stories to highlight points of inspiration for young readers. The goal of this book is simple: to encourage more girls, from a wider range of backgrounds, to pursue political leadership. Seeing more women reach top political roles is a critical and necessary step toward achieving gender equality in our world.

The patriarchy-smashing team at Second Story Press share this goal. In particular, this project would not have been possible without the leadership (and patience) of Jordan Ryder and her team. Erin Della Mattia enormously improved the book through brilliant editorial guidance. The stunning illustrations by Dane Thibeault brought the words and stories to life. Thoughtful perspectives and wise feedback from several people shaped how these stories are told: Susan Graham, Lee Helmer, Arielle Kayabaga, Ovi Kulkarni, Shahzia Khan, and eleven-year-old Parker Ritchie.

Finally, Jesse and Flora Helmer give this project (and life) meaning and purpose, filling me with hope that progress is always possible.

About the Author

Kate Graham researches, writes, speaks, and teaches about politics. She holds a PhD in Political Science from the University of Western Ontario and teaches at Huron University and Western University in London, Ontario, Canada. Kate is the creator and host of *No Second Chances* (NoSecondChances.ca), a Canada 2020 podcast about the rise and fall of women in Canada's most senior political roles. This project inspired Kate to write *Govern Like a Girl* (the Canadian edition), *No Second Chances*, and *Run the World Like a Girl: International Women Leaders*.

Kate lives with her partner, Jesse, and daughter, Flora, in London, Ontario, Canada.